MW00951005

Reproducible Activities

Nonfiction
Reading Comprehension

Grades 1-2

By
Theresa Gerig
Kris Robinson-Cobb
Glenda Sible Shull

Cover Design by
Matthew Van Zomeren

Inside Illustrations by
Peggy Falk

Published by Instructional Fair • TS Denison
an imprint of

 **McGraw-Hill**
Children's Publishing

About the Authors

Theresa Gerig has taught for twenty-four years in the elementary school setting. She received her bachelor's and master's degrees in education from Indiana University. She lives near Fort Wayne, Indiana, and is presently teaching third grade.

Kris Robinson-Cobb received her bachelor's and master's in education from Indiana University. She is a certified media specialist. She has taught in the elementary grades for twenty-one years.

Glenda Sible Shull is a graduate of Manchester College and Indiana University. She is an author and an elementary teacher.

Credits

Authors: Theresa Gerig, Kris Robinson-Cobb, and
        Glenda Sible Shull
Inside Illustrations: Peggy Falk
Cover Design: Matthew Van Zomeren
Project Director/Editor: Mary Rose Hassinger
Editors: Alyson Kieda, Sara Bierling
Graphic Layout: Tracy L. Wesorick

McGraw-Hill
Children's Publishing

A Division of The McGraw·Hill Companies

Published by Instructional Fair • TS Denison
An imprint of McGraw-Hill Children's Publishing
Copyright © 2002 McGraw-Hill Children's Publishing

Send all inquiries to:
McGraw-Hill Children's Publishing
3195 Wilson Drive NW
Grand Rapids, Michigan 49544

Nonfiction Reading Comprehension—grades 1–2
ISBN: 0-7424-0218-5

2 3 4 5 6 7 8 9 PHXBK 07 06 05 04 03

Name _____

Olympic Games

The world's best athletes are in the Olympic Games. These games are held once every four years. They are held in a different country each time.

Before the games start, there is a special ceremony. During this ceremony, a runner lights the Olympic Flame. This runner uses a torch that was first lit in the country of Greece. Many runners carry this torch until it is in the country where the games are being held. The Olympic Flame burns until all of the games are over. It is a symbol of peace.

The Olympic symbol is five rings linked together. There are three rings on the top and two rings on the bottom. They stand for Africa, Asia, Australia, Europe, and the Americas. The colors of the rings are blue, black, red, yellow, and green. Every country in the games has at least one of these colors in its flag.

Directions: Color these rings to look like a famous Olympic symbol. Start on the left. Color the top rings first.

Color the first ring blue. Color the second ring black.

Color the third ring red.

On the bottom row, color the first ring yellow.

Color the second ring green.

Directions: After reading page seven do this activity.

Color the torch in Greece yellow.

Follow the torch path to Australia. Color a pattern of yellow, red, yellow, red, until you reach Australia.

Color the Olympic Flame yellow.

Write the name of the country where the torch is first lit. _____

Write the name of the country where the Olympic Games are being held in this picture. _____

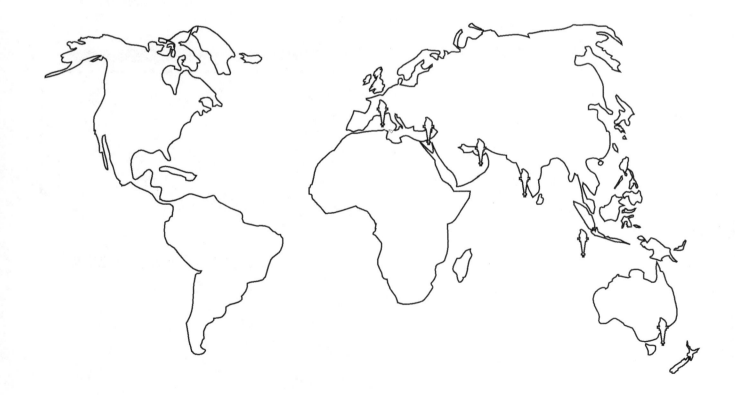

Name _____

Bears

Directions: There are many kinds of bears. Each kind of bear is special. Read these stories about bears and follow the directions.

The black bear is usually black. It can be blue-gray, brown, or even white. The black bear spends most of the winter sleeping in a cave or hollow log. Baby bears are born in January or February. The black bear likes to eat berries, honey, and meat. **Look below. Color the black bear black. Write one fact about the bear below it.**

The polar bear is a white bear. It lives in the cold Arctic. The bottoms of the polar bear's feet are covered with hair. The hair helps keep the bear's feet warm and helps it walk on the ice without slipping. The polar bear is a good swimmer. It likes to eat fish, sea birds, and other meat. **Look below. Color the polar bear white. Write one fact about the bear below it.**

The grizzly bear is usually brownish with silver tips on its fur. The grizzly bear eats small animals, fish, berries, honey, and plants. In the winter it sleeps in a den. Baby bears are born in January or February. A grizzly bear can live to be between fifteen and thirty-four years old. **Look below. Color the grizzly bear brown. Write one fact about the bear below it.**

_____   _____   _____

_____   _____   _____

Name _____

Bike Safety

Riding a bike can be fun. Children like to ride bikes. Grownups like to ride bikes. Sometimes we ride bikes on the sidewalk. Sometimes we ride bikes in the street. No matter how old you are or where you ride your bike, there are rules you should follow. These rules will help keep you safe. Riding a bike should be fun and safe.

Directions: Draw a line to match the safety rule with the picture.

1. Always ride in single file.

a.

2. When you need to cross a street, walk your bike.

b.

3. Hold your left hand straight down away from your side when you are going to stop or slow down.

c.

4. Do not have two people on a bike with only one seat.

d.

5. Do what traffic lights and signs tell you to do.

e.

Name _____

Killer Whales

Killer whales are sea mammals. They are black and white. They eat meat such as fish and seals. They also will eat other whales. Killer whales are the only type of whale that kills and eats other whales. Killer whales often go with other killer whales to hunt sea animals. They can swim faster than almost any other mammal in the sea.

Some killer whales are kept by people. These whales are very smart. Some have even been trained to do tricks. They do not often hurt the people who care for them.

Directions: Read each sentence. Draw a circle around the word that makes the sentence not true. Write the word from the story beside the sentence to make the sentence true.

1. Killer whales are birds. _____

2. Killer whales live in the mountains. _____

3. Killer whales are black and blue. _____

4. Killer whales eat plants. _____

5. Killer whales are sleepy, so they can be taught to do tricks.

_____

Name _____

Foxes

Directions: Read the story carefully. Then match the definition of each word by writing the correct letter in the foxes below.

A fox looks almost like a dog. It has a pointed <u>snout</u>, or nose on its face. It has a long bushy tail.

Foxes often live in <u>burrows</u>, or holes in the ground. They hunt at night. They use their <u>senses</u> such as sight, hearing, and smell. These help them to <u>locate</u>, or find, food. Foxes eat <u>rodents</u> such as mice and squirrels. They also eat birds, rabbits, and frogs.

A fox is very <u>clever</u>, or smart. It is hard to catch. It plays tricks on dogs that chase it. The fox will sometimes run through water. Then the dog will no longer be able to follow its <u>scent</u>, or smell.

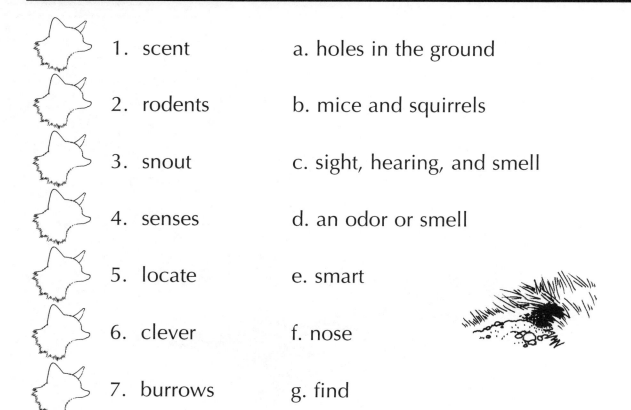

1. scent   a. holes in the ground

2. rodents   b. mice and squirrels

3. snout   c. sight, hearing, and smell

4. senses   d. an odor or smell

5. locate   e. smart

6. clever   f. nose

7. burrows   g. find

Name _____

Bird Beaks

All birds have beaks. The beaks of birds are shaped differently because of the food they eat.

The roseate spoonbill is a bird that has a spoon beak. It is shaped like a spoon to scoop up shellfish and water insects found in shallow water.

Birds such as sparrows and finches have cracker beaks. These are strong, short beaks that can crack the hard shells of seeds that they like to eat.

A spear beak is found on herons. This beak is long and pointed so that the birds can catch fish and frogs along the shore.

Flamingos like to eat plants and shellfish. They have strainer beaks. These beaks are long and curved. They have combs that strain out the mud and keep the flamingos from swallowing it.

Directions: Under each picture, write the name of the bird and the kind of beak it has. Then write what kind of food each bird likes to eat.

1.

bird _____

beak _____

food _____

2.

bird _____

beak _____

food _____

3.

bird _____

beak _____

food _____

4.

bird _____

beak _____

food _____

Name _____

Boats

Directions: Read about each boat, then answer the riddles below.

There are many kinds of boats.

A rowboat is a small boat that is moved through water by pulling on oars. Oars are long poles that have one wide, flat end.

A houseboat is a boat that has rooms where people can live. People can eat and sleep on a houseboat. They can live on a houseboat for a long time.

A tugboat is a small boat. It is very strong. It can push or pull boats that are much bigger.

A fireboat is a boat made to help put out fires. A fireboat has water and hoses. It uses them to put out fires on other boats or buildings along the water.

A sailboat is a boat that is moved by the wind. A sailboat has one or more sails, or sheets, made of strong cloth. The wind fills the sails and moves the boat along.

1. I am moved by the wind. What am I? _____

2. I help put out fires on water and along the shore.
   What am I? _____

3. I pull big boats in the water. What am I? _____

4. You can take me on a small lake. I move with oars.
   What am I? _____

5. You can live on me for a long time. What am I?

   _____

Name _____

Wart Hogs

Wart hogs live in Africa. Wart hogs get their name from the <u>warts</u>, or bumps, on their faces. They look a lot like pigs.

Wart hogs have <u>tusks</u>, or long pointed teeth. The tusks stick out from the sides of their mouths. They use the tusks to <u>root</u>, or dig up the ground looking for food. They eat almost anything.

Wart hogs also use their tusks to fight. They usually do not choose to fight. They will <u>flee</u>, or run away, with their tails sticking up in the air. They hide in <u>thickets</u>, or bushes, in the day and come out at night to eat.

Directions: Write a word from the box below that could take the place of the underlined words in the sentences.

root	tusks	flee	thickets	warts

1. Wart hogs have <u>pointed teeth</u>. _____

2. Wart hogs <u>dig for food in the ground</u>. _____

3. Wart hogs live in <u>bushes</u>. _____

4. Wart hogs have <u>bumps</u> on their faces. _____

5. Wart hogs <u>run away</u> from danger. _____

Name _____

Snow

Snow is small white flakes of frozen water that fall from the sky. Snowflakes have six sides. No two snowflakes are the same.

Snow falls to the ground when the air is cold. It usually falls in the winter. If the ground is warm, the snow melts or turns back into water. If the ground is cold, the snow will often stay. When a lot of snowflakes fall quickly, it is called a snowstorm.

Sometimes the wind blows hard when it is snowing. The snow blows and makes it hard to walk and drive. When the wind blows hard and it is snowing, it is called a blizzard. During a blizzard, snow can be blown into big piles called snowdrifts.

During and after a blizzard, some people become snowbound. Snowbound people cannot drive cars or fly airplanes. Children who are snowbound usually have the day off from school.

Directions: Read the story. Look at the words that are underlined. Find the meanings of the words below. Draw a line to match the word on the left with its meaning on the right.

1. snow
2. melts
3. snowstorm
4. blizzard
5. snowdrifts
6. snowbound

a. snow blown into big piles
b. people cannot drive cars or fly planes
c. small white flakes of frozen water
d. turns back into water
e. a lot of snowflakes fall quickly
f. the wind blows hard when it is snowing

Name _____

Flags

A flag is often made of cloth. It has different colors and can have symbols or pictures on it. Some cities have flags. States and countries also have flags. Groups like the Boy Scouts and Girl Scouts have flags, too.

Directions: Read the descriptions of some flags on pages 17 and 18. Match the description to one of the flag pictures below. Write the name of the flag under its description. Color the flag to match the description.

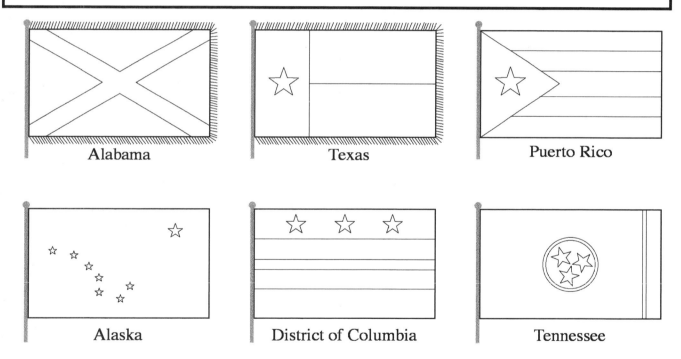

Alabama   Texas   Puerto Rico

Alaska   District of Columbia   Tennessee

1. This flag has three rectangles. The top rectangle is white. The bottom rectangle is red. The rectangle on the left is blue with a white star. It has gold fringe around it. To whom does this flag belong?

_____

2. This flag has seven gold stars that stand for the Big Dipper. It has another gold star in the corner that stands for the North Star. The rest of the flag is blue. To whom does this flag belong?

_____

3. This flag has a blue triangle with a white star in it. It has five stripes. The top stripe is red. The next stripe is white. The next stripes are red, then white, and then red. To whom does this flag belong?

_____

4. This flag has three red stars across the top on a white background. The stripe under this is red. The next ones are white, then red, then white. To whom does this flag belong?

_____

5. This flag has a blue circle in the middle with three white stars in it. The outside of the circle is white. It is in the middle of a big red rectangle with a thin strip of white and a strip of blue on the edge. To whom does this flag belong?

_____

6. This flag is white. It has a large red cross that looks like an X. There is gold fringe around the outside of the flag. To whom does this flag belong?

_____

Name _____

Bird Facts

Directions: Read about some interesting birds. Use what you read to complete page 20. Write the name of each bird under its picture. Then write two facts you learned about each bird.

A bird is an animal with feathers. All birds have wings, but not all birds can fly. Some birds that cannot fly are the ostrich, the emu, the penguin, and the kiwi.

The ostrich is the largest bird. A male African ostrich may grow to be eight feet (2.4 meters) tall. It might weigh 300 pounds (140 kilograms). The ostrich is also the fastest running bird. It can run about 50 mph (80 kph) for short distances. Ostriches cannot fly.

The emu is also a large bird that cannot fly. It is about five and a half feet (1.7 meters) high. It weighs 100 pounds (4.5 kilograms). Emus like to eat farm crops, fruits, and green plants.

Penguins cannot fly, but they are good swimmers. Their wings are like flippers used for swimming. They live where it is very cold. They spend most of the time in water. Penguins like to eat fish.

Kiwis have very tiny wings with brown feathers. They are about the size of a chicken. Kiwis are the only birds that have nostrils at the tips of their long bills. The nostrils help them find worms, insects, and berries. Kiwis come out at night and hide during the day.

Name _____

1.

2.

bird _____

fact 1 _____

fact 2 _____

bird _____

fact 1 _____

fact 2 _____

3.

4.

bird _____

fact 1 _____

fact 2 _____

bird _____

fact 1 _____

fact 2 _____

Name _____

What Is It?

You can throw it. You can kick it. You can bat it. You can roll it. It can be hard. It can be soft. It may have air inside. What is it? It is a ball.

Balls are used in more than thirty sports and games. Some of these are **baseball**, **football**, **basketball**, and **soccer**.

People think that small round stones were used long ago instead of balls. Later, people began making balls stuffed with animal hair, cork, string, and yarn.

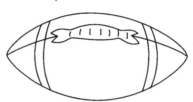

Directions: Read the story. Look at the words in dark print. These are the names of sports played with balls. Write the name of the correct sport after its description below.

1. In this sport, you can kick the ball, throw the ball, and run with the ball. The ball is not round.

   _____

2. In this sport, you hit a small round ball with a club. You try to hit the ball into a hole. _____

3. In this sport, the ball is round and has air inside it. You bounce it and shoot it through a hoop.

   _____

4. In this sport, you throw and catch the ball. You also hit the ball with a wooden stick. _____

Name _____

Hermit Crabs

The hermit crab lives in a shell in or near the ocean. It does not make its own shell. It moves into a shell left by another sea animal. As the hermit crab grows, it gets too big for its shell. It will hunt for a new shell. It will feel the new shell with its claw. If the shell feels just right, the crab will leave its old shell and move into the bigger one. It might even take a shell away from another hermit crab.

Directions: Read about hermit crabs. Use what you learn to finish the sentences.

1. This story is mostly about the _____.

2. The hermit crab lives _____.

3. When it gets too big for its shell, it will _____.

4. The crab will feel the shell with its _____.

5. It might take a shell away from _____.

Name _____

The Statue of Liberty

The Statue of Liberty is a symbol of the United States. It stands for freedom. It is the tallest statue in the United States.

The statue is of a woman wearing a robe. She is holding a torch in her right hand. She is holding a book in her left hand. She is wearing a crown. The Statue of Liberty was a gift from the country of France.

Each year, people come from all over the world to visit the statue. Not only do they look at it, they can also go inside the statue. There are stairs that lead all the way up to the crown. Inside the crown, people can stand and look out over New York City.

Directions: Read the facts above. Then read each sentence below. If it is true, put a **T** on the line. If it is false, put an **F** on the line.

_____ 1. The Statue of Liberty is a symbol of the United States.

_____ 2. People cannot go inside the statue.

_____ 3. The statue was a gift from Mexico.

_____ 4. People stand in the crown and look over New York City.

_____ 5. It is a very short statue.

_____ 6. The woman statue has a torch in her right hand.

_____ 7. People come from all over to see the statue.

Name _____

Venus Flytraps

Many insects eat plants. There is one kind of plant that eats insects. It is the Venus flytrap. The Venus flytrap works like a trap. Each leaf is shaped like a circle. The circle is in two parts. When the leaf closes, the two parts fold together. The leaf has little spikes all the way around it. Inside the leaf there are little hairs. If an insect touches the little hairs, the two sides of the Venus flytrap leaf will clap together. The spikes will trap the insect inside. The Venus flytrap will then eat the insect.

Directions: Read about the Venus flytrap. Then read each sentence below. If it is true, color the Venus flytrap.

Each leaf is shaped like a square.

The Venus flytrap is a plant.

The Venus flytrap's leaves have little hairs inside.

The sides of the leaf clap together.

The Venus flytrap is an insect.

Name _____

Sticklebacks

Sticklebacks are small fish. They have small spines along their backs. The spines keep other fish from trying to swallow them.

Stickleback fish are odd because the male builds the nest for the eggs. He makes the nest out of water plants and sticks. He makes it in the shape of a barrel and glues it together. He uses a threadlike material from his body to glue the nest together.

When the nest is ready, the mother fish comes. She lays her eggs and goes away. The father stays by the nest and guards the eggs. After the eggs hatch, he stays with the baby fish for a few days. If other sea animals try to eat the baby sticklebacks, he will fight them. He keeps the baby fish safe until they can care for themselves.

Directions: Read about the stickleback fish. Use the story to help pick the correct answers to fill in the blanks. Circle the correct answer.

1. The story is mostly about _____.

    spines   enemy sea animals   stickleback fish

2. The stickleback is unusual because _____.

    the female lays eggs   the male builds a nest   the eggs are in the nest

3. The nest is made of _____.

    mud and grass   water plants and sticks   string and glue

4. If an animal tries to eat the baby fish, the stickleback father will _____.

    fight it off   swim away   jump out of the water

Eagles

Eagles are large birds. They eat small animals such as mice and rabbits. Eagles make their nests in high places such as the tops of trees. Their nests are made of sticks, weeds, and dirt. Eagles can live in the same nest for many years.

The mother eagle lays one or two eggs each year. When she sits on the eggs, the father eagle brings her food. Baby eagles are called eaglets.

Directions: Read about eagles. Then circle the correct ending to each sentence below.

1. Eagles are

   large dogs.   large birds.

2. Eagles eat

   small animals.

   plants and trees.

3. Eagles

   build a nest each year.

   live in the same nest for many years.

4. The mother eagle lays

   one or two eggs.

   three or four eggs.

5. Baby eagles are called

   igloos.   eaglets.

Name _____

Seals

Seals live in the oceans and on land. They eat different kinds of sea animals, such as fish, shrimp, squid, and krill. They are very good swimmers. They use their flippers to help them move in the water and on the land. They talk to each other by making barking sounds.

Directions: Read the facts above. Then answer each question using complete sentences.

1. What do seals eat? _____

   _____

2. For what do seals use their flippers? _____

   _____

3. Where do seals live? _____

   _____

4. How do seals talk? _____

   _____

Name _____

Animals in the Winter

Directions: Read about some special animals in winter. Then answer the questions on page 29 using your own words.

In some parts of the world, winter means cold weather, icy winds, frozen ponds, and snow. When it turns cold, people put on warm coats or snowsuits. Animals cannot do that. What do animals do when winter comes?

In winter some animals leave their homes. They go where they can find food. They go where it is warmer. They stay until the spring comes. Then they return home. This is called *migration*. Butterflies and some birds migrate south. Whales migrate to warm waters in winter.

Other animals do not leave their homes in winter. These animals go into a deep sleep called *hibernation*. Animals such as groundhogs sleep in their underground homes. Their bodies use stored fat to stay alive. Frogs and turtles hibernate in the muddy bottoms of ponds. Their skin breathes the air that is trapped in the mud. They become cold and stiff. They do not eat all winter.

Some animals do not migrate or hibernate. Their bodies change to help them to stay alive. Some animals grow extra fur that traps air, keeping them warm. Foxes grow thick fur. Some animals' fur changes color to hide from other animals. The snowshoe rabbit's fur changes from brown to white.

Directions: Use the story on page 28 to answer these questions.

1. What is the difference between migration and hibernation?

_____

_____

_____

_____

2. Some animals do not migrate or hibernate. Tell how these animals stay alive in winter.

_____

_____

_____

_____

_____

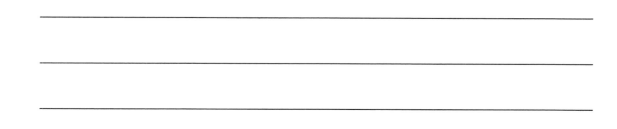

Name _____

Uncle Sam

U.S. stands for United States. They are also the initials for a symbol of the United States—Uncle Sam.

Long ago there was a real Uncle Sam. His name was Sam Wilson. During the War of 1812, Sam Wilson gave meat to the United States soldiers. He called himself Uncle Sam. He stamped U.S. on his barrels of meat. The soldiers were glad to have the meat. They began to say they were fighting for Uncle Sam.

People wrote about Uncle Sam and drew pictures of how they thought he looked. Today when we see pictures of Uncle Sam, we see a man with a white beard. He is dressed in a coat with long tails. He wears a tall hat with stars and red, white, and blue stripes. Sometimes people dress up like Uncle Sam and walk in parades.

Directions: Read the story. Then read the sentences below. Mark the true sentences with a **T**. Mark the false sentences with an **F**.

_____1. Uncle Sam wears red, white, and blue.

_____2. Uncle Sam is the President of the United States.

_____3. Uncle Sam was a real man.

_____4. Sam Wilson helped the United States.

_____5. Uncle Sam Wilson was a baker.

_____6. Uncle Sam wears a tall hat.

Name _____

Icebergs

There are big sheets of ice on the South Pole and near the North Pole. Sometimes large pieces break off these sheets. These pieces float out into the ocean. They are called icebergs.

Icebergs can be huge. They can be as big as a mountain. Often only a little of the iceberg can be seen above the water. Most of the iceberg is below the water. Ships that cannot see icebergs below the water are sometimes in

danger. The Titanic was a ship that bumped into an iceberg. The iceberg made a hole in the Titanic, and it sank.

Most icebergs never harm ships. They float in the ocean until they come to warmer water. There, they begin to melt. When the iceberg melts, it becomes part of the ocean water.

Directions: Underline the correct word to complete each sentence.

1. Sometimes chunks of ice float out into the (river, ocean).

2. Only a little bit of the iceberg can be seen above the (water, clouds).

3. The Titanic was a(n) (airplane, ship).

4. Icebergs come from sheets of ice on the South Pole and near the (North Pole, shore).

5. A large chunk of floating ice is called an (ice cube, iceberg).

Name _____

Sun Bears

A sun bear is the smallest of all bears. It is usually black with an orange or white circle on its chest. The orange mark on the bear's chest looks like a sun so people long ago began to call it the sun bear. Sun bears have very long claws. They use their claws to help dig for insects and small animals. The claws also help them climb trees. They build stick nests in trees. Sun bears sleep in the day and hunt at night. They eat insects, small animals, and honey. They are sometimes called Malayan bears.

Directions: Circle the best word to complete each sentence.

1. The sun bear is the (largest, smallest) of all bears.

2. Sun bears are usually (black, brown).

3. The orange circle on the bear's chest looks like a (sun, balloon).

4. The bear's (fur, claws) help it climb trees.

5. Sun bears build nests of (straw, sticks).

6. The bears sleep (at night, in the day).

7. They are sometimes called (grizzly, Malayan) bears.

Name _____

Silkworms

Directions: Read about silkworms. Then use what you learned to help answer the questions on page 34.

Did you know that the shirt you are wearing right now may have been made with the help of a caterpillar? A silkworm is really a caterpillar, not a worm. These caterpillars make silk threads which are used to make silk fabric.

The life cycle of a silkworm begins in springtime. Pale yellow eggs are laid by the female silk moth. After about twenty days, the eggs hatch into tiny silkworms. These silkworms feed on mulberry leaves. They grow to be about three inches (8 cm) long and one inch (2.5 cm) thick. After about twenty-five days, the caterpillars are ready to spin their cocoons. Using silk glands near their mouths, they use one thread of silk to spin their cocoon. This takes about four days. During the next fourteen days, the caterpillar, wrapped in its cocoon, changes into a silk moth. The moth lays eggs and the cycle begins again.

Silkworms can be raised on farms. The caterpillars spin cocoons. Then the cocoons are heated to keep the caterpillars from changing into moths since moths break the thread when they leave the cocoon. Growers don't want the thread to be broken. The long threads are then woven together to make them strong. These threads are then used to make silk fabric.

> **Directions:** Use page 33. Circle the correct answers to the questions.

1. Circle the correct life cycle of a silkworm.

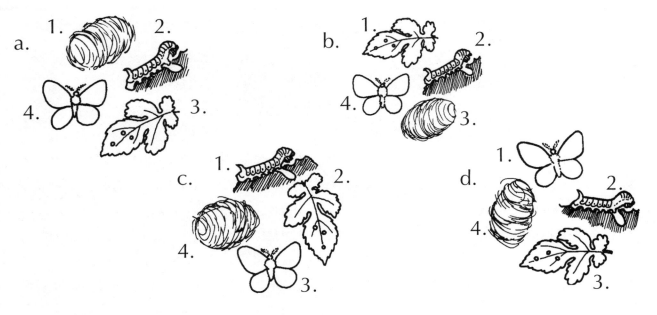

2. About how long does it take for the eggs from a silk moth to hatch?

    a. 20 days　　b. 25 days　　c. 3 days　　d. 14 days

3. Why are the cocoons heated when silkworms are raised on farms?

    a. to keep them warm
    b. so the silkworms won't change into moths
    c. so the moths will break out sooner
    d. to make the silk threads stronger

4. For what does a silkworm use its silk thread?

    a. to make silk fabric
    b. to spin its cocoon
    c. to eat mulberry leaves
    d. to help it move quickly

Name _____

Apples

Apples grow best where there are four seasons in the year. In the spring, apple trees will have white blossoms, or flowers, and small green leaves growing on their branches. The blossoms drop off and tiny green apples start to grow. In the summer, the tree branches fill with small apples that grow and grow. In the fall, the big apples are ready to be picked. Leaves start to drop off the branches. In the winter, the apple tree will rest. It does not grow any leaves or apples. It is getting ready to grow blossoms and apples again in the spring.

Directions: Draw a picture to show how an apple tree changes with each season.

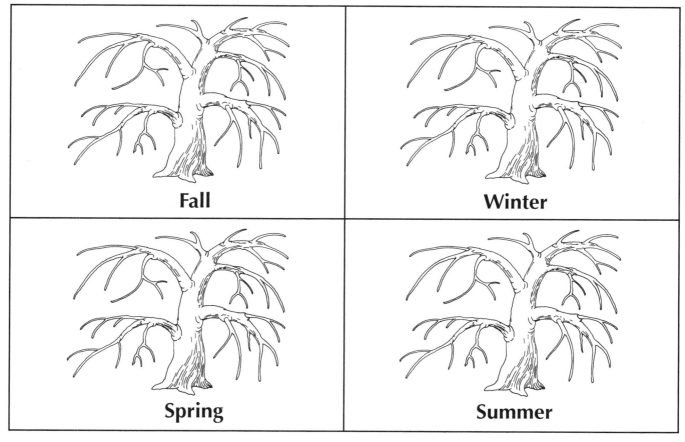

Fall

Winter

Spring

Summer

Name _____

Hurricanes

Hurricanes form during the warmest months of the year. The hurricanes that come to the Americas usually start over the Atlantic Ocean or Gulf of Mexico. The sun heats the ocean, and starts to evaporate. The warm, moist air rises, and cool air rushes to replace it. The moist air is pushed up where clouds form. The clouds start touching and swirling around in a circle. The circle forms a doughnut-shaped storm, or hurricane, that can be hundreds of miles across.

The center of this doughnut-shaped storm is called the "eye" of the hurricane. The eye has calm winds. If a person were to look straight up inside the storm, he would see blue sky. The eye of the hurricane is about fifteen miles (24 km) across.

Directions: Think about what you just read about hurricanes. Answer the questions below.

1. In what months do you think most hurricanes form? _____

_____

2. Why don't people living in Indiana, Kansas, and Idaho have to worry about hurricanes?

_____

3. How would knowing about hurricanes help someone who is planning a trip to the Atlantic Ocean?

_____

4. Do you think there are hurricanes at the North Pole? _____

Why? _____

Name _____

Ounces, Pounds, Tons

In the United States, ounces, pounds, and tons are used to measure weight. An ounce is the smallest common unit of measurement. A candy bar weighs just a few ounces. A newborn kitten might weigh 4 ounces (113.4 grams).

Sixteen ounces make one pound. Right after you were born, a nurse weighed you. You might have weighed 7 pounds (3.18 kg). Some people buy potatoes, bananas, and carrots by the pound.

Two thousand pounds make a ton. This is the largest unit of weight. A dump truck hauls tons of dirt, rocks, or sand. Railroad cars and ships move tons of grain or coal across the land and water. An elephant might weigh 7 tons (6.35 metric tons).

Measurement by weight is a part of your life. How much do you weigh?

Directions: Circle ounces, pounds, or tons to tell how each would be measured by weight.

1. Three small pieces of candy

    ounces   pounds   tons

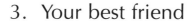

2. Your family car

    ounces   pounds   tons

3. Your best friend

    ounces   pounds   tons

4. A goldfish in a bowl

    ounces   pounds   tons

Name _____

Louis Braille

Louis Braille was three years old when he had an accident that blinded him. When Louis turned fifteen, he developed a method that helped blind people to read. This method is called Braille. It is used by placing your fingers on raised dots. The dots are arranged in different ways to stand for letters of the alphabet and numerals.

Directions: Use the Braille letters shown to decode the message below.

i   c   d   n   r   a   b   e   l

____   ____   ____   ____

____   ____   ____   ____

____   ____   ____   ____   ____   ____   ____

Name _____

 # Unusual Fish

Cave fish are whitish in color. They grow to be about 5 inches (13 cm) long. They live in caves and underground rivers. Some have eyes, but they cannot see. Others have no eyes at all.

Flying hatchetfishes are a shining silver color. They grow to be about 4 inches (10 cm) long. They swim near the top of the water. They jump out of the water and fly through the air to catch insects.

A walking catfish can live in and out of the water. It can move from one lake to another by walking on land. It has no legs so it pushes itself along with its tail, using its strong fins to move the front of its body.

Directions: Make up a new kind of fish. Use the blanks to describe your fish. Then draw a picture to match your description.

_____
name of your fish

_____
size

_____
color(s)

_____
where it lives

_____
characteristic

_____
characteristic

Name _____

Teddy Bear

The teddy bear was named for a real man. The man's name was Theodore Roosevelt. His nickname was Teddy. He was a President of the United States.

Teddy liked the outdoors. He liked to hunt and fish. One day when he was hunting bear with some friends, they saw a bear cub. His friends wanted Teddy to shoot the bear cub. Teddy would not shoot the little bear. Newspapers wrote stories about Teddy and the bear. Toy makers liked the story. They began to make soft toy bears and called them teddy bears.

Directions: Answer the questions below.

1. Why do you think Teddy did not want to shoot the baby bear?

    _____

    _____

    _____

    _____

2. Do you think a teddy bear is a good toy? Tell why or why not.

    _____

    _____

    _____

    _____

Name _____

Magpies

The magpie is a noisy bird. It likes to copy sounds other birds make. These birds can be tamed. They can even be trained to speak simple words.

The magpie cannot be trusted by other birds. It will often steal food right from their nests.

Magpies often build their nests in thorny bushes for protection. The nests are big with a dome-shaped top. A hole is left in one side for the magpies to get in and out of the nest. They lay five to ten greenish-blue eggs that have brown and tan spots. Magpies may live about twelve years.

Directions: Read about magpies, then write the answer to each question.

1. If you were going to choose a bird for a pet, would you choose a magpie? Why or why not?

   _____

   _____

2. Do you think other birds should build their nests near a magpie's nest? Why or why not?

   _____

3. How do thorn bushes protect a magpie?   _____

   _____

4. Why do you think a magpie's nest is completely closed except for an opening in the side?

   _____

   _____

Name _____

The Good Doctor

Directions: Read about what a veterinarian does. Then answer the questions on page 43.

When you do not feel well or have hurt yourself, you can tell your parents. If they cannot help you, they can take you to a doctor. The doctor will check you. He or she might ask you questions. The doctor will tell you what you need to do to get better. You might have to take medicine. You might have to stay home from school so you do not share your illness with others. You might have to rest or do special exercises. Soon you will feel better.

When pet, farm, or zoo animals get sick or hurt, they cannot actually tell anyone. Animal owners must watch their pets to know when they are hurt or sick. When a pet is sick, the owner will take it to a special animal doctor. This is a veterinarian, or vet. If a large farm or zoo animal is ill, the veterinarian may visit it.

A veterinarian goes to school and studies how to help or treat sick and hurt animals. This is just like your doctor who went to school to learn how to help you.

A vet has a very hard job. Animals cannot tell the vet where it hurts or how it feels. The vet must examine the animal. Often the animal does not understand that the vet wants to help. The animal doctor will ask the owner questions to help find out what is wrong. The vet will tell the animal owner what they need to do to help the animal get better. They might have to take medicine. Sick animals might have to stay away from healthy animals so others do not get sick. They might have to rest or do special exercises. Soon the animal should feel better.

Name _____

Directions: Think about what a veterinarian does and answer the questions. Use the story on page 42.

1. How are a doctor and a veterinarian alike? _____

_____

_____

_____

2. How are a doctor and a veterinarian different? _____

_____

_____

_____

3. How are treating a sick person and a sick animal alike? ____

_____

_____

_____

4. How might treating a baby be like treating an animal? _____

_____

_____

_____

Name _____

Hedgehogs

The hedgehog is a small animal. It has a small head that is pointed. At the tip of the point is a funny little nose. On its underside, the hedgehog has soft fur. On its back, it has sharp hairs called spines. When the hedgehog becomes afraid, it rolls into a ball. All you can see are the spines. When it does this, other animals will not try to harm it.

Directions: Use the story about hedgehogs to help fill in the missing words on the lines below.

1. The hedgehog is a small _____.

2. His head is _____.

3. On its underside, the hedgehog has soft _____.

4. On its back, it has sharp hairs called _____.

5. When it is afraid, it rolls into a _____.

Name _____

Walking Sticks

The walking stick got its name because it looks like a stick that walks. It looks so much like a stick you can hardly see it as it sits on a twig or branch.

The walking stick is an insect. It has a long, thin body with six thin legs. If a leg breaks, it can grow a new one. The walking stick walks very slowly when it moves. It eats leaves from many kinds of trees. It eats mostly at night. During the day, the walking stick sits quietly and looks like a stick so birds will not see it and eat it.

Directions: Use the story about the walking stick to help fill in the missing words on the lines below.

1. The walking stick got its name because it looks

   like a _____ that _____.

2. A walking stick is an _____.

3. A walking stick walks very _____.

4. A walking stick eats _____.

5. If a leg breaks, it _____ a new one.

Name _____

Classifying

Sometimes you want to put things in groups. One way to put things in groups is to sort them by how they are alike. When you put things together that are alike in some way, you classify them.

You can classify the things in your room. In one group you can put toys and fun things. In the other group, you can put things that you wear.

Directions: Look at the words on the bedroom door. Put the toys and playthings in the toy box. Put the things you wear in the dresser drawers.

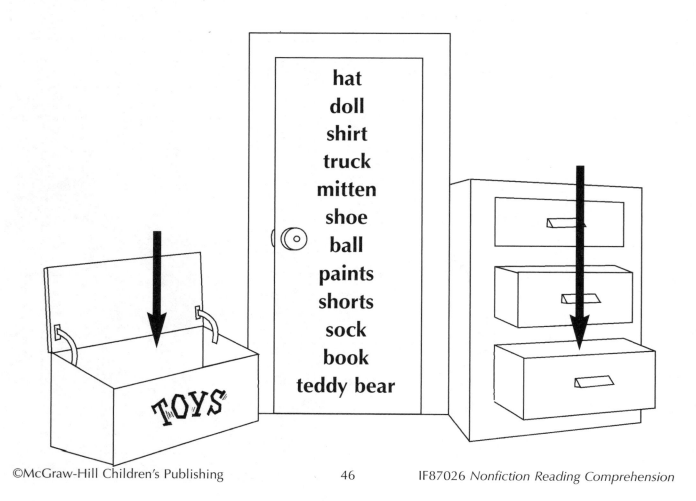

hat
doll
shirt
truck
mitten
shoe
ball
paints
shorts
sock
book
teddy bear

TOYS

Name _____

 # Baby Animal Names

Many animals are called special names while they are young. A baby deer is called a fawn. A baby cat is called a kitten.

Some young animals have the same name as other kinds of baby animals. A baby elephant is a calf. A baby whale is a calf. A baby giraffe is a calf. A baby cow is a calf.

Some baby animals are called cubs. A baby lion, a baby bear, a baby tiger, and a baby fox are all called cubs.

Some baby animals are called colts. A young horse is a colt. A baby zebra is a colt. A baby donkey is a colt.

Directions: Use the story about baby animal names to do the chart below. Write the kind of animal that belongs with each special baby name.

calf	cub	colt

Name _____

Directions: Look at the pictures of the mother animals and their babies. Write the name of the baby on the line. Use page 47 if needed.

---

a.

_____

b.

_____

c.

_____

d.

_____

e.

_____

f.

_____

Name _____

Shrews

A shrew (*shroo*) is a small animal. It looks like a mouse with a sharp, pointed nose. This animal is sometimes for a mouse. It has tiny eyes and ears. Its body is covered with short dark hair. A shrew moves very fast. A shrew eats all day. The shrew's long, pointed nose can fit into tiny holes to find the insects and worms it eats.

The shrew lives in fields, woodlands, gardens, and marshes. Shrews are harmless to humans. They are helpful in gardens because they eat grubs and other insects. The smallest shrew weighs as little as a United States penny.

Directions: After reading about the shrew, put an **X** on one word that does not belong in each group.

1. small   large   tiny

2. bugs   corn   insects

3. move   run   sleep

4. bird   mouse   dish

5. fast   quick   water

6. sharp   pointed   hair

7. nickel   penny   rain

8. garden   fields   sun

Winter's Sleepers

Directions: Read about hibernation. Then complete page 51.

As days grow shorter and it gets colder, some animals get ready for their winter's sleep. This winter's sleep is called *hibernation*. Scientists do not know all the secrets of hibernating animals. They do know enough to put hibernating animals into two groups. One group is called "true hibernators." The other group is called "light sleepers."

True hibernators go into a very deep sleep. To get ready for this long winter's sleep, true hibernators will eat and eat so they become fat. As these animals sleep, their body temperature drops below normal. If the animal gets too cold, it will shiver to warm itself. The breathing of true hibernators slows so much that they hardly seem to breathe at all.

True hibernators are animals such as woodchucks, some ground squirrels, the jumping

mouse, brown bat, frogs, and snapping turtles.

Light sleepers include skunks, raccoons, the eastern chipmunk, and the grizzly bear.

Some light sleepers will store up food to have during winter while others will eat and become fat. A big difference between light sleepers and true hibernators is that the light sleeper's body temperature drops only a little, and its breathing only slows. These animals are easy to wake and may even get up if the temperature warms. They then go back to sleep when it becomes colder again.

Directions: Read all of the word groups, then place them under the correct hibernation type. Use the story on page 50.

will shiver to warm itself
body temperature drops a little
hardly breathes at all
seems more dead than alive
moves about and then goes back to sleep
breathing only slows
easily awakens
stores up food
body temperature drops far below normal
uses body fat while sleeping

True Hibernator

_____

_____

_____

_____

_____

Light Sleeper

_____

_____

_____

_____

_____

Name _____

Birds

There are <u>many</u> kinds of birds. The cardinal is a <u>red</u> bird. The cardinal lays <u>three</u> or <u>four</u> eggs. The brown-headed cowbird is <u>black</u> with a <u>brown</u> head. The hummingbird is a very <u>small</u> bird. It lays <u>two</u> eggs. The bald eagle is a <u>large</u> bird. It is brown with a <u>white</u> head. The bald eagle lays from <u>one</u> to <u>four</u> eggs. Bluebirds are <u>blue</u> with <u>orange</u> or light <u>blue</u> breasts. The bluebird lays up to <u>six</u> eggs.

Directions: In the story above the underlined words are adjectives. Put these describing words in the nests where they belong.

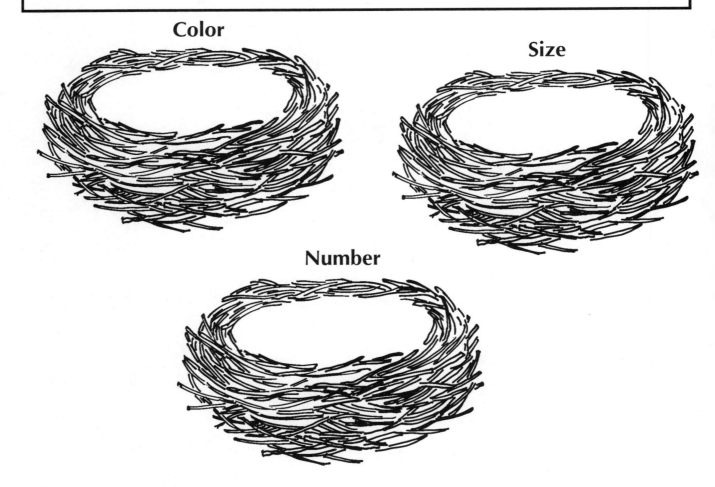

Color

Size

Number

Name _____

All Animals

There are many kinds of animals. Three kinds of animals are mammals, birds, and reptiles.

Mammals have fur or hair. Baby mammals drink milk from their mothers' bodies. A whale is a mammal.

Birds are the only animals that have feathers. A robin is a bird.

Reptiles have scaly skin. Most reptiles lay eggs on the land. An alligator is a reptile.

Directions: Read the sentences below. Is the animal in the sentence a mammal, bird, or reptile? Put an **M** on the line if it is a mammal, a **B** if it is a bird, or an **R** if it is a reptile.

____1. Maggie brushes her horse's coat.

____2. The turtle lays its eggs in the sand.

____3. Adam cleans the feathers from his pet's cage.

____4. The baby penguin hides in its father's feathers to stay warm.

____5. The piglets drink their mother's milk.

____6. The scaly skin on the snake is dry.

____7. A blue jay has blue feathers.

____8. The bunny pulls fur from her body to build a nest.

Name _____

Five Senses

Directions: Read this story about the senses. Do the activities on page 55.

As you use your eyes to read this, you are using one of your five senses. You are using your sight. Your sense of sight lets you see faces, places, shapes, letters, and words. Your sight helps you see beautiful things and helps keep you safe.

Bells ringing, children singing, and your mother calling you to dinner all use the sense of hearing. Your ears catch sound waves that travel through the air and you hear them.

Your sense of hearing warns you with a beep-beep that a truck is backing up. A phone rings and you hear it. Could it be a friend calling?

Your sense of smell lets you know that a pizza is cooking without you even seeing it. Your nose smells the fresh sheets on your bed and lets you know that your dog has been playing in the rain or with a skunk.

You use your tongue for tasting. Foods can taste salty, sweet, sour, or bitter. Your sense of smell and taste work together so you can enjoy food. Dill pickles or tangy oranges are tasty treats. Cotton candy and popcorn are also tasty treats.

Your largest sense organ is your skin. Your sense of touch is found in your skin. You can feel smooth, soft, rough, sharp, hot, and cold. Velvet is a smooth touch. Sandpaper is rough. Snow is cold, and cotton balls are soft.

Your five senses help to keep you safe and help you enjoy life.

Name _____

Directions: Draw a line to match the sense to the body part that works with it.

eyes   taste

ears   smell

nose   sight

tongue   hearing

skin   touch

Directions: List three of your favorites under each sense. An example is given.

Taste _pretzel_____

_____

Smell _baking cookies_____

_____

Sight _Mommy_____

_____

Hearing barking dog_____

_____

Touch _cold snow_____

_____

Name _____

Penguins

A penguin is a bird that cannot fly. Its wings look and act like flippers. Penguins are very good swimmers and spend a lot of time in the water. White belly feathers and short black feathers on their backs make it hard to spot them in the water. They waddle when they walk. Most wild penguins live in the southern part of the world.

Female penguins lay one to three eggs. The male carries the eggs on his feet and covers them with rolls of body fat to keep them warm. A baby penguin is called a chick when it is hatched. Most penguins can live for almost twenty years.

Directions: After reading about penguins, decide if each statement is a fact or an opinion. Write **F** for fact and **O** for opinion.

_____ 1. A penguin is a beautiful bird.

_____ 2. A penguin is a bird that cannot fly.

_____ 3. Penguins are good swimmers.

_____ 4. Baby penguins are called chicks.

_____ 5. Female penguins are good nest builders.

_____ 6. It is fun to watch penguins swimming.

_____ 7. Bird watchers like to watch penguins.

_____ 8. A penguin may live for twenty years.

Name _____

Starfish

A starfish is not really a fish. It is an animal. It belongs to a group of animals that have skin that is tough and covered with sharp bumps called spines.

Starfish live in the ocean.

Most starfish have five "arms" going out from the main body. This makes them look like stars. The mouth of a starfish is on the underside of its body. A starfish can eat in two different ways. It can take food in through its mouth and eat it. It can also eat by pushing its stomach out of its mouth and wrapping it around the food.

If an arm breaks off the starfish, it can grow a new one.

Directions: Read the statements. Decide if each is a fact or an opinion. Write **F** for fact and **O** for opinion.

_____ 1. It would be fun to feel a starfish.

_____ 2. A starfish would be a good pet.

_____ 3. If a starfish "arm" breaks off, it can grow a new one.

_____ 4. Starfish look pretty.

_____ 5. Starfish live in the ocean.

_____ 6. Starfish have tough skin with spines.

Name _____

Figs

Fig is the name of a fruit and of the plant the fruit grows on. The plant can look like a bush or like a tree. Fig plants grow where it is warm all year long.

The fig fruit grows in bunches on the stems of fig plants. Some figs can be picked two times each year.

They can be picked from old branches in June or July. They can be picked from new branches in August or September.

Many people like to eat figs. They can be eaten in fig cookies or in fig bars. They can be canned or eaten fresh. Sometimes figs are dried.

Directions: Color the fig **red** if the sentence is a **fact**. Color the fig **blue** if the sentence is an **opinion**.

 1.   A fig is a plant and a fruit.

 2.   The fig tree is very pretty.

 3.   Fig plants don't grow where it is very cold.

 4.   Figs grow in a bunch.

 5.   You can pick figs two times each year.

 6.   Figs taste very good.

 7.   You can eat figs in many ways.

 8.   The best way to eat a fig is in a fig cookie.

Name _____

Neighbors to the South

To the south of the United States is the country of **Mexico**. The language spoken in Mexico is **Spanish**. The money used is the **peso**. Mexico has modern cities as well as ancient ruins. Many people visit Mexico each year.

Most Mexicans wear clothes like those worn in the United States. People in the smaller villages may wear more traditional clothing such as wide-brimmed hats called sombreros. Sombreros help protect the wearer from the hot sun. Ponchos, or cloaks, are worn in cold weather.

The most important crop grown in Mexico is **maize,** or corn. Many Mexicans also eat beans seasoned with hot chili peppers. Some Mexican foods we enjoy are tacos, enchiladas, and tortillas.

A celebration, or festival, in Mexico is called a **fiesta**. Music and dancing are important parts of a fiesta. A popular folk dance is the Mexican hat dance. One of the best known fiesta traditions is breaking open a piñata. Piñatas are hollow animal shapes filled with candy, toys, and fruit.

Directions: Draw a line to connect each word with its correct meaning.

1. A Mexican celebration   peso

2. Language spoken in Mexico   maize

3. Country south of the United States   fiesta

4. Money used in Mexico   Mexico

5. Important Mexican crop   Spanish

Name _____

Ships

A ship is a large boat that travels the oceans. Ships carry people and goods from place to place.

A ship has many parts. The **bow** is the front part of a ship. The **stern** is the back part of a ship. Goods are kept in **holds** below the decks. The sails of a ship are held by poles called **masts**. Sometimes there is a **crow's nest** on a mast. This is a place where a sailor can look out over the water.

An important part of a ship is the **helm**. This is the ship's steering wheel. It is used to make the ship turn in different ways.

Directions: Use the Word Bank to help label the parts of the ship.

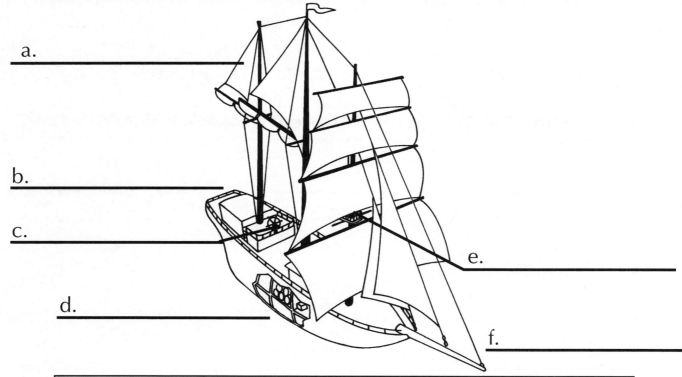

a. _____

b. _____

c. _____

d. _____

e. _____

f. _____

Word Bank					
bow	mast	helm	holds	stern	crow's nest

Name _____

Totem Poles

Totem poles are tall poles **carved**, or cut, from trees. They were often made by Native Americans to tell stories about a family. These stories would tell how the family lived with **nature**, such as the animals, the forest, and the plants around them.

After the poles were carved, they were sometimes painted. Then the tribe would hold a **potlatch**, or feast. They would put the totem poles near their homes. Some would be used to greet **guests**, or friends. Others were made for people who had died.

Directions: Look at the words in the box below. Match each word with a meaning. Write its letter in the totem pole next to the correct meaning.

a. guests   b. potlatch   c. totem poles   d. carve   e. nature

____ feast

____ cut

____ tall, carved poles that tell stories

____ the forest, animals, and plants

____ friends that visit

Name _____

Daisy

Once there was a girl named Daisy. Daisy did many things as she was growing up. She rode horses. She drew pictures and loved to sculpt. She acted in some plays.

After Daisy grew up, she started the Girl Scouts. Girl Scouts do many of the things Daisy did as a girl. They play games and enjoy outdoor activities such as hiking.

Daisy's real name was Juliette Gordon Low. It was her wish that the girls in Girl Scouts be helpful to people and make the world a better place.

Directions: Find the words in the story above that will fit in this crossword puzzle.

Across

2. _____ can join the Girl Scouts.

3. Juliette Gordon Low was called _____.

4. Daisy rode _____.

5. Daisy acted in _____.

Down

1. Girl Scouts make the world a better _____.

2. Daisy started the _____ _____.

Name _____

Saguaro Cactus

Directions: Use this story about cactuses to help complete the crossword puzzle on page 64.

Don't touch that cactus plant! The pointed <u>needles</u> on a cactus can hurt. Cactuses grow in <u>deserts</u> where little rain falls. Cactus <u>roots</u> quickly drink up rainwater. The water is saved in the ribs and grooves of the cactus. These <u>expand</u>, get larger, like an accordion, depending on how much water is stored. Then the ribs and grooves contract, becoming smaller as the water is used.

The <u>saguaro</u> (*suh GWAH roh* or *suh WAH roh*) is the largest cactus in the United States. It is also called a giant cactus. It can grow as tall as 60 feet (18 meters). This would be as tall as a six-story building.

Branches on the cactus turn up. They look like <u>arms</u>. In May and June, greenish-white flowers grow at the ends of the arms. They bloom at <u>night</u>. Later, the flowers turn into purplish-red, <u>egg</u>-shaped fruit. The ripe fruit splits open. Desert creatures will eat the fruit. It can also be used to make jelly or syrups.

Name _____

Directions: Use the underlined words in the story on page 63 to fill in the crossword puzzle.

Across

3. to get larger

6. the largest cactus in the United States

7. where a cactus grows naturally

Down

1. these drink up fallen rainwater

2. what the cactus has that might hurt

4. time of day the cactus blooms

5. what the cactus branches look like

8. the shape of the cactus fruit

Name _____

Vampire Bats

Directions: Read about vampire bats. Use the bold words to help finish the crossword puzzle on page 66.

There are over 900 kinds or species of **bats** in the world. They are the only flying mammal in the world. One bat is the **vampire** bat. Vampire bats are found in Central and South America.

The vampire bat is not very big. They are about 2 to 2.5 inches (5 to 6.25 cm) long. The **wingspan**, or distance from one wing tip to the other, can be 12.5 to 14 inches (25 to 35 cm).

Vampire bats are **nocturnal**. This means they sleep during the day and are active at night. When flying at night, bats use echolocation to help them "see" in the dark. **Echolocation** means that the bat sends out squeaks or clicks. When these sounds reach an object in the bat's path, they bounce off, and the sound echoes travel back to the bat. This lets the bat know where the object is, its size, and how fast it is moving.

Vampire bats have **heat sensors** on their noses. This helps them find the area on their prey where the blood is close to the skin. Vampire bats usually feed on sleeping horses, cattle, chickens, or turkeys.

The bat doesn't suck blood with **fangs**, sharp-pointed teeth, but licks the blood, from a small **round** cut, like a cat would drink milk. The **saliva** of the bat stops the blood from clotting so the bat can drink all it needs, which is about two **tablespoons**. The vampire bat eats only one time each night.

The **roost**, or place where the bats rest during the day, usually has a strong, unpleasant smell because of the digested blood. Vampire bats roost in caves, hollow trees, old wells, mine shafts, or old buildings. They roost alone, in small groups, or in **colonies** of over 2,000 bats.

Directions: Use the bold words in the story on page 65 to help finish the crossword puzzle.

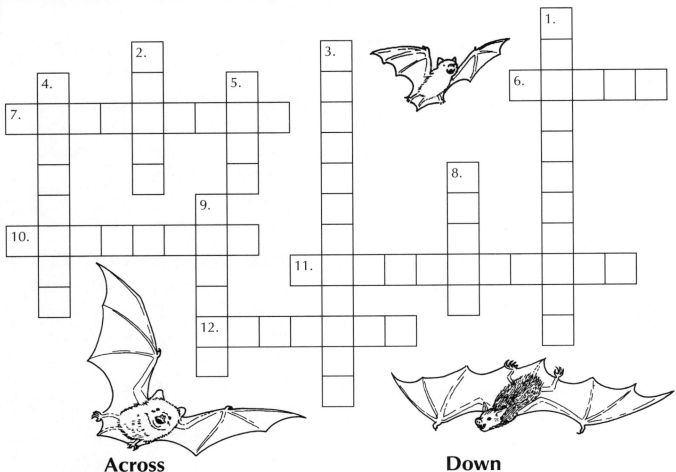

Across

6. sharp, pointed teeth

7. sleeps during the day, active at night

10. distance between wing tips

11. bat needs two of these full of blood each day

12. only bat that drinks blood

Down

1. found on the bat's nose

2. shape of cut vampire bats make

3. helps bat see in dark

4. large group of bats

5. only mammals that fly

8. place bats rest

9. stops blood from clotting

Manatees

Directions: Read about manatees. Use what you learn to finish page 68.

Manatees are sometimes called sea cows. They are mammals. They must come to the water's surface to breathe air.

The West Indian manatee lives along the coast of Florida. It is shy and gentle. Manatees are herbivores. This means that they eat only plants. Baby manatees are called calves. They drink mother's milk like all mammals.

Habitat is the place where something lives. Habitat is the space that has food, water, air, and shelter. The manatee habitat is changing so fast that manatees are in danger. They are on the endangered animals list.

The warm, shallow waters, or lagoons, that manatees prefer are being filled in with dirt to create more land. The manatees have less fresh water to live in and drink. The water is muddy, so light cannot reach the plants. Without light, plants can't grow.

Speedboats are another danger to manatees. The whirling blades of boat propellers can hurt the manatees. Caution signs slow some boats down, but not all.

Pollutants are harmful things that are sometimes in the water. They can cause manatees to become sick and weak. Manatees must have clean, warm water to live.

Manatees cannot live for very long when the water gets too cold. Manatees migrate or travel to warm waters using the same routes every year. With dams and canals being built and even some river courses being changed, manatees become confused, lost, and can even die.

Where manatees once lived, there are now people, boats, mud, and pollutants. The habitat of the manatee is disappearing and so are the manatees.

Name _____

Directions: Read the story on page 67. Use what you read to help match the words to their meanings. Draw straight lines from the word to the definition.

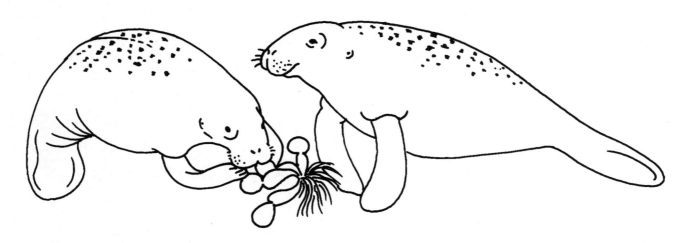

1. migrate

2. mammals

3. habitat

4. disappearing

5. survive

6. harmless

7. pollutants

8. herbivores

a. will not hurt you

b. eat only plants

c. breathe air, drink mother's milk

d. the living space that includes food, water, air, and shelter

e. return to the same place by the same route year after year

f. going away; leaving

g. able to live

h. harmful, unclean things put in water

Name _____

Kites

Directions: As you read this story about kites, think about words that are opposites. Remember, opposite words are words whose meanings are very different from each other. *Hot* and *cold* are opposites. *In* and *out* are also opposites. When you find a word that is opposite to a word in a kite below, write the word on that kite.

Kites are special toys. Some are black and white. Some kites are big and some are little. Some are round and some are square.

Kites go up and down in the air as the wind blows. They can go very high, or they can fly low over the trees.

It is very fun to play with kites.

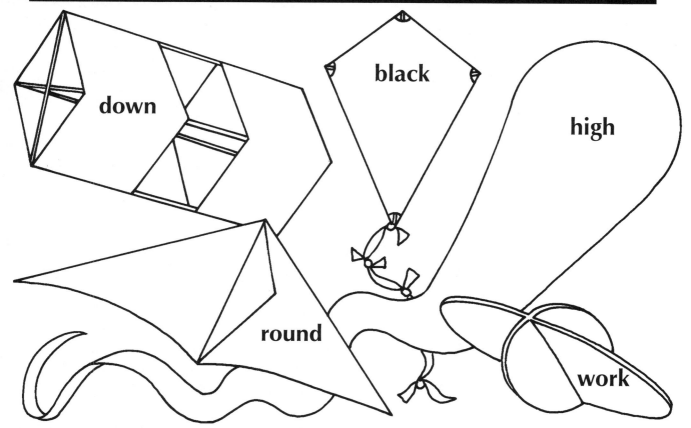

down

black

high

round

work

Name _____

Bark

Bark is what you see on the outside of a tree. Some bark is **thin** and **smooth**. Other bark is **thick** and **rough**. Bark can be different colors. Many trees have **dark-colored** bark. Others have **light-colored** bark.

There are two layers of bark. The **outside** layer of bark protects the tree. This is the part we see. The **inside** layer is used to store and carry food from the **top** of the tree to the **bottom**.

Many years ago, people used bark to make shelter, clothing, and canoes. The bark of some trees is used for special things. It can be used to make chewing gum, rubber, and a spice called cinnamon. If you are **sick,** you might take cherry cough medicine to help make you **healthy**. Cherry cough medicine is also made from bark.

Directions: After reading about tree bark, find words in the tree that are opposite to words outside the tree. Draw lines to match them.

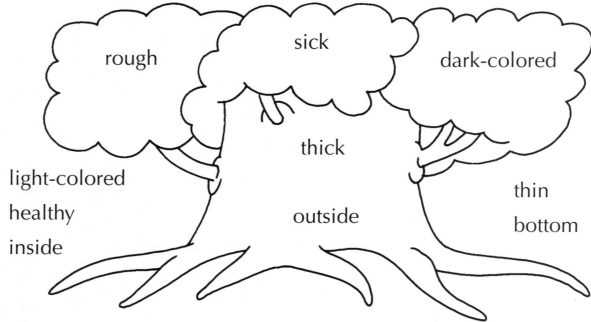

rough

sick

dark-colored

thick

light-colored

healthy

inside

outside

thin

bottom

Name _____

Ducks

Ducks are birds. They live in or near water. Ducks have short legs. They have webbed feet that help them swim. Ducks have flat beaks called bills. They have two kinds of feathers. Down feathers are very soft. They grow next to the ducks' skin and keep ducks warm. The outer feathers keep ducks dry.

Baby ducks are called ducklings. Ducklings hatch or come out of eggs. The mother duck lays her eggs in a nest. The father duck is called a drake.

Directions: Read about ducks. Circle the word that best completes the sentence below. Color the eggs that have details from the story.

This story is mostly about (feathers, ducks).

Ducks have two kinds of feathers.

Father ducks are called drakes.

Ducks are birds.

Ducks say, "Quack, quack."

People eat duck eggs.

Baby ducks are called ducklings.

Name _____

Animal Migration

Directions: Read these facts about animal migration. Use what you read to help you do the activity on page 73.

1. Many animals migrate. They move from one place to another. Some move because they cannot find food. Others move to find a better place to raise their young.

2. Many birds migrate south in the winter. They cannot find enough food where it is cold. They fly south where it is warm. There they find food for the winter. When winter is over, they fly back north.

3. Some whales live in the cold waters of the Arctic. They spend the summers there. When it begins to freeze, the whales swim to warmer seas. They have their babies in warm water because the babies do not have a thick layer of blubber to keep them warm.

4. Salmon are fish that are usually born in freshwater streams. They migrate to the ocean where they eat shrimp, squid, and small fish. When they are ready to lay eggs, they return to the streams where they were born.

Directions: Use the facts on page 72. Put an **X** next to the main idea of each paragraph. Write one detail that supports the main idea.

Paragraph 1

_____ Some animals move because it is cold where they live.

_____ Many animals migrate to find food and to raise their young.

_____

Paragraph 2

_____ Birds migrate south so they can find food.

_____ When winter is over, birds fly north.

_____

Paragraph 3

_____ Whales migrate to warm waters to raise their young.

_____ Baby whales don't have blubber.

_____

Paragraph 4

_____ Salmon migrate from fresh water to the ocean.

_____ Salmon eat shrimp, squid, and small fish.

_____

Name _____

Happy Birthday

Directions: Read the story about birthdays. The underlined words are compound words. On each cake below, write a compound word. On each candle on the cake, write the words that make the compound word.

Underline <u>Everyone</u> has a birthday. A birthday is the day a person is born. <u>Sometimes</u> people have a party to celebrate their birthday.

Birthday parties started long ago. People once thought there were good spirits and bad spirits. When <u>someone</u> had a birthday, friends and family came together. They wanted to keep away bad spirits.

Today children and <u>grownups</u> have birthday parties. People bring gifts. Often, ice cream and cake are served.

Name _____

Tomatoes

Directions: Before reading about tomatoes, complete the first two columns of the KWL chart on page 76. When you finish reading, write the new facts you have learned about tomatoes in the last column.

There are many kinds of tomatoes. There are red ones, yellow ones, orange ones, and even purple ones! They come in many sizes and shapes. Some are small and round like a grape. Others are as big and round as a peach. Some are not round at all.

You can grow tomatoes in your garden. You can plant seeds or buy small plants from the store. Tomato plants get little yellow flowers on them that change into small tomatoes.

Tomatoes can be eaten in many ways. You can cook them, dry them, or eat them fresh. You can put them in soup, eat them on pizza, or put a slice on your sandwich. Tomatoes are very good for you.

Name _____

Directions: Use the chart below with the story on page 75.

What I know about tomatoes:	What I want to know about tomatoes:	What I learned about tomatoes:

76 IF87026 *Nonfiction Reading Comprehension*

Name _____

Skunks

Directions: Before reading about skunks, finish the first two columns of the chart below. When you finish reading the story, write the new facts you've learned in the last column.

A skunk is a small mammal with short legs and a bushy tail. The skunk is best known for the bad-smelling liquid it can spray from two glands called scent glands. Before the skunk sends out this spray, it warns its enemies by raising its tail or stamping its feet.

Skunks eat insects, mice, and eggs. They live in underground holes, called burrows. Some also live under barns or other buildings.

Skunks are helpful to people because they eat the insects that harm farmers' crops. Skunk fur is used to make clothes. Some people keep skunks as pets after they remove the scent glands.

What I know about skunks:	What I want to know about skunks:	What I learned about skunks:

Name _____

Sleep

Directions: Before reading about sleep, finish the first two columns of the KWL chart on page 83. When you finish reading, write the new facts you have learned in the last column.

Everybody sleeps. It gives the body a chance to rest. When you sleep, your mind and body are working hard. Your brain sorts and stores the things you have done, seen, and heard.

Without sleep, you would not grow. A special chemical is put into your body while you sleep. It tells your body to grow. This same chemical helps your body to heal. Cuts, bruises, and muscles repair while you sleep.

Babies need the most sleep. Everything is new to a baby. He has a lot of experiences to sort out and remember. A baby also needs a lot of sleep because he is growing so fast.

Children up to twelve years of age need ten to twelve hours of sleep. Teenagers need nine to ten hours of sleep. Most adults need an average of seven to eight hours.

Without enough sleep, it is hard to think and remember things. Sometimes it is hard to talk, run, jump, write, or draw like you want to. Without sleep, you may get cranky or grouchy. You are also more likely to get sick.

Sleep, cont.

Name _____

Directions: Use the chart below with the reading on page 82.

What I know about sleep:	What I want to know about sleep:	What I learned about sleep:

take forty-winks z-z-z-z-z-z-z-z

©McGraw-Hill Children's Publishing   83   IF87026 *Nonfiction Reading Comprehension*

Name _____

Verbs

Directions: Remember that a verb is a word that tells what a person, place, or thing is doing. The verb is the action word. Read the poem below and use it to fill in each animal's action.

Doing Things
Birds fly,
Rabbits hop,
Dogs run,
Mothers mop,
Monkeys climb,
Mice hide,
Horses walk,
And baby kangaroos ride.

Birds _____

Rabbits _____

Dogs _____

Mothers _____

Monkeys_____

Mice _____

Horses_____

Baby kangaroos_____

Name _____

Eating Right

Directions: Read about good eating habits. Then look at the foods listed below. Write the names of the healthy foods on the lunch sack. Write the unhealthy foods on the trash can.

Some foods are good for you. They help your body grow. They help your teeth and bones become strong and healthy. Fruits and vegetables are good foods for you. Milk and things made with milk are good for you, too. Nuts, crackers, and bread make good and healthy snacks.

Some foods are not as helpful to your body. They do not give your body the important things it needs to grow. Foods made with a lot of sugar such as candy and cookies are not as good for you. They are not good for your teeth. Foods with a lot of salt and fat also are not good for your body.

Healthy Foods

lollipop

potato chips

milk

carrot

soda pop

apple

cookies

bread

cake

cheese

eggs

Unhealthy Foods

Name _____

Alexander Graham Bell

Directions: Read about a great inventor. Then find the six words in the box that best describe Bell. Write them on the lines below.

Alexander Graham Bell did many great things. We know him most for inventing the telephone. But Alexander had many other talents. He could play music by ear when he was a very young boy. He taught music and speech. He also taught the deaf just as did his father in Scotland.

While Alexander was teaching, he became interested in electricity. He and his friend Thomas Watson did many experiments before the telephone was invented.

Alexander stayed busy after inventing the telephone. He created a research laboratory for the deaf. He invented an electric probe used by doctors. He worked on ways to locate icebergs by using echoes. He did many experiments with kites.

creative	strong	smart
clumsy	funny	musical
busy	talented	
afraid	hard-working	

_____   _____

_____   _____

_____   _____

Name _____

Ida Lewis

Directions: Read about Ida Lewis. Then use the Word Bank to finish each sentence about Ida.

Ida Lewis lived many years ago. She lived at the Lime Rock Lighthouse with her family. Her father was the lighthouse keeper. When he became sick, Ida took over his job.

Ida was a hard worker. She lit the lamp in the lighthouse each night. She filled it with oil and cleaned it each day. Ida was also very strong. She was good at rowing a boat. She rowed her brothers and sisters from the island to the mainland to school each day.

In the same small boat, Ida saved many people from drowning. The people were so thankful they gave her a boat. The boat was named the *Rescue*. Even the President and vice president came to meet her. When Ida died, the lighthouse was given a new name. It was called Ida Lewis Lighthouse.

Word Bank			
brave	loving	hard worker	strong

1. When Ida took care of her family she felt _____.

2. When Ida rowed her boat in a storm to help someone she

    was _____ and _____.

3. When Ida filled the lamp with oil, cleaned it, and lit the

    lamp she was being a _____.

Name _____

Finding a Book

MAGIC MADE EASY · SKINNY MINNIE · SNAKES, TURTLES, LIZARDS · BATS GO HUNTING · Horses and You · JUMPING · FLOWERS · Fun outdoors · CRAFTS for KIDS · Pet Care · SCARY STORIES · MARBLES & JACKS · How to Hula-hoop · Insects, Insects, etc. · Sauerkraut, Pickles and Preserves · YOUR PET RAT ILLUSTRATED · GARDENING · Training your dog · Make your own DOLLHOUSE · DANCE AROUND THE WORLD · Computer Wizards · Abraham Lincoln · X-C BIKING · KIDS COOK · Elephants · DINOSAURS · ART CARS · Guide to Fishes · Skateboard King

When you go to the library, you may want to find a certain book. You can look for a special book in two different ways.

The first way to find a book is by using the book's title. Use the first letter of the title to find the book. If you are looking for *Charlotte's Web*, you would look under C for *Charlotte's*. To find *Arthur's Pet Business*, you would look under A for *Arthur's*.

Another way to find a special book is by using the author's name. Look under the first letter of the author's last name. If you are looking for *Panda the Wizard* by Oda Taro, you would look under T for Taro. To find *Grandma and the Pirates* by Phoebe Gilman, you would look under G for Gilman.

Directions: Write the letters you would use to find these books. The first one is done for you.

1. *Tuesday* by David Wiesner   Title __T__ Author __W__
2. *Danny and the Dinosaur* by Syd Hoff   Title _____ Author _____
3. *Far North* by Will Hobbs   Title _____ Author _____
4. *Dazzle the Dinosaur* by Marcus Pfister   Title _____ Author _____
5. *Just Me and My Mom* by Mercer Mayer   Title _____ Author _____
6. *Leo the Lop* by Stephen Cosgrove   Title _____ Author _____
7. *Lucille* by Arnold Lobel   Title _____ Author _____
8. *Where the Wild Things Are* by Maurice Sendak   Title _____ Author _____

Name _____

Encyclopedias

Directions: Read about encyclopedias. Then look at the set of encyclopedias. Decide which volume you would use to look for the information below. Write the letter(s) of the volume on the line. The first one is done for you.

An encyclopedia is a book that helps you learn about many things. It can help you answer questions that you have about the world.

Some encyclopedias come in sets. Each book in the set is called a volume. Information is put in the books alphabetically so you can find information more quickly. If you wanted to know about elephants, you would look in volume E for elephants. If you wanted to know the different parts of a plant, you would look in volume P under plant. Information about how to play football would be in volume F.

A	B	C	D	E	F	G	H	I	J-K	L	M	N-O	P	Q-R	S	T	U-V	W-X Y-Z

__T__ 1. names of different trees

_____ 2. where bears live

_____ 3. three kinds of rocks

_____ 4. what the Mayflower looks like

_____ 5. dolls around the world

_____ 6. state flags

_____ 7. how a newspaper is made

_____ 8. where the game of tennis began

Name _____

Growing Bananas

Bananas grow where it is hot and damp. They are grown on large farms. After they are picked, they are shipped all over the world.

Banana plants grow in rich, sandy soil. After about four weeks, leaves begin to sprout. These leaves keep growing and growing until they are 6 to 10 feet (2 to 3 meters) long.

When the plant is about ten months old, a large bud with purple leaves forms. Many small flowers grow under these leaves. The flowers change into tiny green bananas.

The bananas grow for four to five months. They are green when they are picked but are usually ready to eat when we buy them.

Directions: Color the banana next to the correct answer to each question.

1. What is the first step in growing bananas?
   a. The leaves grow 6 to 10 feet long.
   b. Small flowers grow under the leaves.
   c. The plants are put in rich, sandy soil.

2. What happens after the bananas grow for four to five months?
   a. They are picked.
   b. Large buds appear.
   c. Leaves begin to sprout.

3. What is the last step when growing bananas?
   a. Tiny green bananas grow.
   b. They are grown on large farms.
   c. They are picked and shipped to other countries.

Jumbo

Children from all over England came to see the new baby African elephant. They fed him apples and peanuts. The elephant grew and grew. His name was Jumbo.

People came from all over to see Jumbo. Children rode on his back in a special seat. Then Jumbo was sold to a circus in the United States.

People in the United States loved Jumbo too. They went to the circus just to see him. They fed him candy and peanuts.

Soon Jumbo went with the circus to Canada. One day Jumbo was walking along a railroad track. He did not hear the train. It hit Jumbo and killed him.

Jumbo is remembered as one of the most loved elephants of all.

Directions: Use the story to number these events in the correct order.

_____ Jumbo went to Canada.

_____ Jumbo was sold to a circus in the United States.

_____ A special elephant was born in Africa.

_____ The elephant was sold to a zoo in London.

_____ Jumbo was walking along a railroad track and was hit by a train.

_____ The elephant's name was Jumbo.

Name _____

Archerfish

Directions: Read the story below. Look at the pictures. Number the pictures in the order in which they happen.

An archerfish lives in fresh water. When the archerfish wants to eat, it swims close to the top of the water. It looks for an insect above the water. When it sees an insect, it shoots or spits out a stream of water. The water hits the insect and knocks it into the water. The archerfish then opens its mouth and eats the insect.

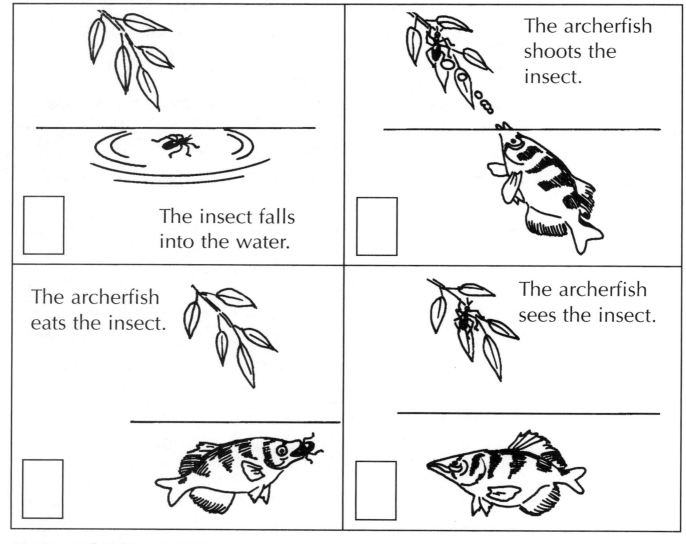

The insect falls into the water.

The archerfish shoots the insect.

The archerfish eats the insect.

The archerfish sees the insect.

Name _____

Compass Rose

North, south, east, and west are directions. A compass rose is a picture that shows these directions on a map. Look at the compass rose below. On the compass rose, the letter N stands for the direction north. The letter S stands for south. The letter E means east. The letter W stands for west.

Directions: Look at the compass rose and the map of the zoo. Answer the questions below.

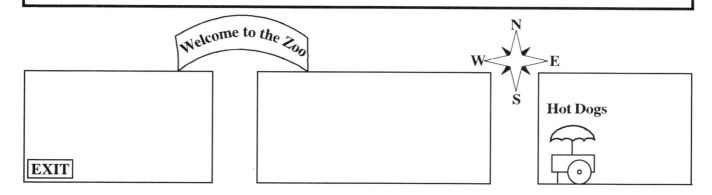

1. What direction do you take from the gate to the elephant area?

   _____

2. What direction do you go from the elephants to the tigers? _____

3. What direction do you take from the tigers to the hot dog stand?

   _____

4. What direction do you take from the hot dog stand to the exit? _____

Name _____

North America

This is a map of North America. North America is one of the seven continents. Find the United States. The United States is a country in North America. Canada and Mexico are also in North America.

Directions: Use the map key and the map of North America to answer the questions below.

1. Name two countries in North America. _____

2. What is the capital of the United States? _____

3. Name two cities in the United States. _____

4. Which ocean is on the west side of North America? _____

5. Which large country is south of the United States?

   _____

6. Name a river in Canada.

   _____

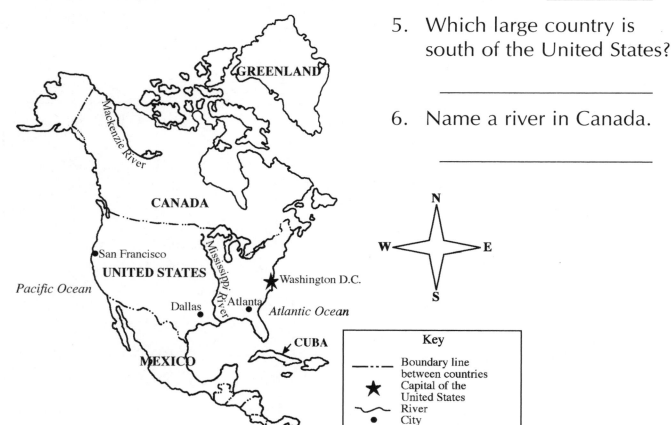

Name _____

Rabbits

Directions: Read about rabbits. Answer the questions below.

Rabbits are small animals. They have short, fluffy tails and long ears that hear very well.

Rabbits eat all kinds of plants. They eat in fields and gardens. Some farmers do not like rabbits because rabbits eat their vegetables and young trees.

When a mother rabbit is ready to have baby rabbits, she digs a small hole. She lines the hole with soft grass and fur from her body. She will have from two to nine babies. Baby rabbits are called kits.

Some people keep rabbits as pets. They keep them in pens or cages. Grains, vegetables, and green grass are good foods for pet rabbits.

1. What is the story mostly about? _____

2. What do rabbits eat?_____

3. Why do some farmers not like rabbits? _____

_____

4. Where does the mother rabbit get the fur for her nest? _____

_____

5. What are baby rabbits called?_____

Name _____

Mantids

A mantid is an insect. We call it a praying mantis. When it hunts, it lifts its front legs and looks like it is praying.

A mantid can grow to be 2 to 5 inches (5 to 13 centimeters) long. It has front legs with sharp hooks to hold its prey. It has short, wide wings. Its body is long and thin.

Mantids are helpful to man because they eat harmful insects. A female mantid might even eat her mate if she is very hungry.

Mantids protect themselves by changing colors. If a mantid is on a green plant, its color might be green. If it is on a brown branch, its color might be brown.

Directions: Use the information in the story to complete these statements.

1. A mantid is called a praying mantis because

   _____.

2. A mantid has sharp hooks on its front legs because

   _____.

3. Mantids can be helpful to man because

   _____.

4. A mantid will eat another mantid if

   _____.

5. A mantid protects itself by

   _____.

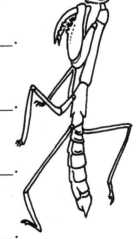

Name _____

Marsupials

Directions: Use words from the story to finish the summary below.

A **marsupial** is an animal that has a **pouch**. The pouch is mostly used to **carry babies**.

When a baby marsupial is born, the tiny animal must **crawl** into its mother's pouch. There it **drinks** its mother's milk and grows. When it is big enough to move on its own, it leaves the pouch. The baby stays close to its mother. If it becomes afraid, it goes back into her pouch.

A **kangaroo**, a **koala**, and an **opossum** are marsupials. These animals do not look alike. They do not eat the same kind of food, but they all have pouches.

The story is about _____. A marsupial is an animal that has a _____. The pouch is used mostly to _____. When a baby is born, it must _____ to its mother's pouch. Inside the pouch, it _____ and grows.

Name three animals that are marsupials.

_____   _____   _____

Name _____

Molting

Some animals lose their outer coverings and grow new ones. This is called molting.

Birds lose their feathers one to three times a year. They lose one feather at a time and grow a new one to take its place. Molting takes four to six weeks.

Snakes molt too. A snake rubs its nose against something hard to break the skin around its head. Then it crawls out of its skin, turning the skin inside out. Young snakes molt more often than older snakes.

Lobsters molt as they outgrow their shells. This happens many times. A lobster's new shell forms inside the old one. The old shell splits and the lobster pulls itself out of the old shell.

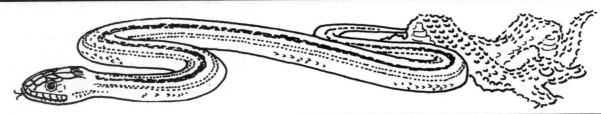

Kind of Animal	How the Animal Molts	Interesting Facts

Name _____

State Birds

Every state has a state bird, flower, and tree. Here are some examples. The sea gull is the state bird for Utah. Sea gulls eat crickets that kill crops grown there. The state tree for Vermont is the sugar maple. Vermont makes maple syrup from these trees. The state flower in Virginia is the flowering dogwood. These flowers bloom on the dogwood tree every spring. You can find each state's tree, flower, and bird by using books in your library.

Directions: This chart lists five state birds and their states. Use the chart to answer the questions below.

Bluebird	Robin	Purple Finch	Pelican	Cardinal
Idaho	Connecticut	New Hampshire	Louisiana	Illinois
Missouri	Michigan			Indiana
Nevada	Wisconsin			Kentucky
New York				North Carolina
				Ohio
				Virginia
				West Virginia

1. What is Michigan's state bird?

   _____

2. What is Louisiana's state bird?

   _____

3. How many states have the cardinal as the state bird?

   _____

4. How many states have the bluebird as the state bird?

   _____

5. Which state has the purple finch as its state bird?

   _____

99

Name _____

Money

Directions: Look at this money chart. It tells what is on the front and back of some United States bills and coins. Use the chart to answer the questions below.

Kind of Money	Front	Back
Penny	Abraham Lincoln	Lincoln Memorial
Nickel	Thomas Jefferson	Monticello
Dime	Franklin D. Roosevelt	Torch, Laurel, and Oak Leaves
Quarter	George Washington	Eagle
Half Dollar	John F. Kennedy	Presidential Seal
Silver Dollar	Dwight D. Eisenhower	Eagle
One Dollar Bill	George Washington	The Great Seal
Two Dollar Bill	Thomas Jefferson	Signing of the Declaration of Independence
Five Dollar Bill	Abraham Lincoln	Lincoln Memorial
Ten Dollar Bill	Alexander Hamilton	U.S. Treasury
Twenty Dollar Bill	Andrew Jackson	The White House
Fifty Dollar Bill	Ulysses S. Grant	U.S. Capitol
One-Hundred Dollar Bill	Benjamin Franklin	Independence Hall

1. Which President is on the quarter and a bill? _____

2. On which coin is John F. Kennedy? _____

3. Which bill has Independence Hall on the back? _____

4. Which Presidents are on both coins and bills? _____

_____

5. Which picture is on both a coin and a bill? _____

Name _____

Candy

Candy is a favorite sweet-tasting food. The main part of most candy is sugar.

There are four main types of candies. They are made differently and contain different things. The best-selling candy is chocolate. The most popular are solid chocolate and chocolate-covered candy bars.

Hard candy is also popular. This candy starts out as a liquid that is boiled. Flavoring and color are added. Then as it cools, it is shaped. A favorite hard candy is the candy cane. These used to be made mostly with peppermint, but now fruit and even chocolate flavoring are used.

Chewy candies are candies such as caramels. These are cooked, cooled, and then cut into pieces or poured into molds and allowed to set.

Whipped candies are nougats and marshmallows. These are syrups mixed with air. Marshmallow bunnies and chicken peeps are examples of these.

In the United States, about five billion pounds (2.3 billion kgs) of candy is sold each year. This is about twenty pounds (9 kgs) per person!

Directions: Take a survey. Ask your friends about their favorite kind of candy. Gather your information using the four main types of candies in the story. Use what you learn to fill in the bar graph on page 102.

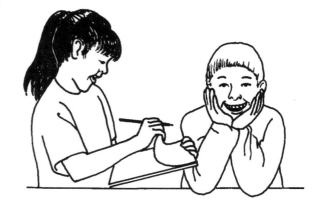

Directions: Make a bar graph to show the results of the survey you took. Use the graph below.

Favorite Types of Candy

	1	2	3	4	5	6	7	8	9	10	11	12	13
Chocolate Candies													
Hard Candies													
Chewy Candies													
Whipped Candies													

1. What kind of candy did most people like?

_____

2. What kind of candy did the least people like?

_____

3. Were any types of candy tied or close favorites?

_____

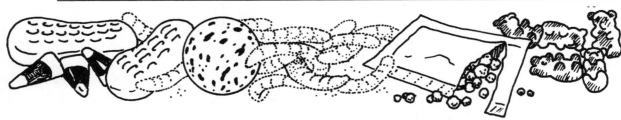

Just for fun, try asking just girls, just boys, or just adults,
and see if the results are the same.

Name _____

Dairy Cows

The milk you drink probably comes from dairy cows. Dairy cows are raised on farms and spend most of their time eating. They eat grass, corn, and other feed. Cows do not chew their food at first. They swallow it whole.

A cow has a large stomach with four parts. When a cow swallows food, it **goes into the first two parts of the stomach**. There, it turns into cud, balls of unchewed food. The cow **brings the cud back into its mouth and chews it**. When it swallows, the food **goes into the third and fourth parts of its stomach**. The food is broken into tiny pieces.

Once the food has gone through all four parts of the stomach, it goes into the cow's blood and **used to make milk**. The milk is kept in the cow's udder until the farmer is ready to milk the cow.

Directions: Fill in the chart. Use the sentences that are bold.

Cows eat grass and other food without chewing it.

↓

↓

The grass turns into cud.

↓

↓

↓

The broken-down food is passed into the cow's blood.

↓

Name _____

 **Tulips**

Tulips are a sign of spring. Unlike many flowers we see in the spring, tulips are planted in the fall.

Many flowers come from seeds. Seeds are planted in soil. The seeds are not planted very deep. Heavy rains can wash the seeds away. Cold weather can kill the new plants as they start to grow. Lots of sunshine and rain are needed to help the plants to grow, blossom, and make new seeds.

Tulips start out as bulbs.

Bulbs are shaped like toy top with a point at one end. When planted about four inches deep, the pointed end must be pointed up toward the ground's surface. Tulip bulbs freeze in the winter. As the soil thaws and warms, so do the bulbs. Sprouts start pushing toward the surface and continue to grow. Sunshine and rain help the tulips grow. Tulips are hardy plants and can even stand a light frost. After a few years, another bulb may start to grow next to the first bulb.

Directions: In the Venn diagram, place the numbers beside the word groups where they belong

1. planted deep in the soil
2. start out as bulbs
3. need soil to grow
4. can be washed away
5. produce seeds
6. need the sun to grow
7. start out as seeds
8. can stand a light frost
9. planted in the fall

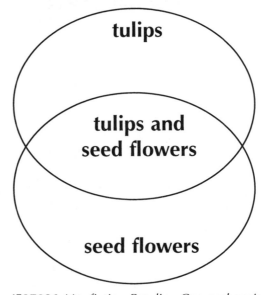

Moths and Butterflies

Moths and butterflies are alike in many ways. They are both insects. Their wings have many tiny colored scales. Both moths and butterflies have long tongues to suck nectar from flowers.

Moths and butterflies are also different. Most moths have antennae that look like little feathers. Butterflies have thin antennae that are bigger at the end. Most moths fly at night, and butterflies fly in the day. When they are not flying, moths sit with their wings out flat. Butterflies that are resting sit with their wings straight up.

Directions: Read about moths and butterflies. Write the numbers of the facts about moths in the top circle, the numbers of the facts about butterflies in the bottom one, and the numbers of the facts that tell about both in the center.

1. have antennae like little feathers
2. have thin antennae that are bigger at the end
3. are insects
4. fly mostly at night
5. sit with wings out flat
6. have tiny colored scales on the wings
7. fly mostly during the day
8. rest with wings up
9. suck nectar from flowers

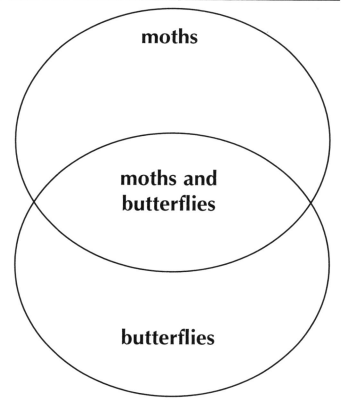

 # Dugongs and Manatees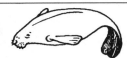

Manatees and dugongs are alike in many ways. They are **mammals**. They are sometimes called sea cows because they are big, slow- moving, and like to **eat sea grass**. They have **two front flippers** and a tail to help them swim. They can be found in the ocean near the coast. They both have **blubber**, a thick layer of fat that keeps them warm.

A manatee has **long whiskers** and **strong teeth**. Its whiskers help it find plants to eat. Its teeth are used to crush tough plants. It has a **rounded tail** to help it swim. When the water gets too cold, the manatee **migrates** to warmer places.

A dugong looks like a manatee except its **tail is flat**. It has **tusks**. It **does not migrate**.

Both animals are **endangered**. Many are killed each year by people. Some are used for their meat and oil. Some are killed by boats. Others get caught in fishing nets and drown.

Directions: Read about dugongs and manatees. Write the bold words from the story in the Venn diagram where they belong.

Dugongs

Dugongs and Manatees

Manatees

Name _____

Prairie Dogs

Directions: Read about prairie dogs. Use what you learn to complete the Venn diagram on page 108.

It looks like a puppy. It acts like a puppy. It can wag its little tail. It makes a yipping sound called a bark. When it sits up it looks like a begging dog. It has tan fur and a black tip on its tail.

What is it?

It is a prairie dog. But prairie dogs are not dogs. Prairie dogs are rodents. Other rodents include mice, beavers, squirrels, and woodchucks.

Prairie dogs live on the prairies. Prairies are big grassy areas with few trees.

Like other rodents, prairie dogs use their long, sharp front teeth for cutting and biting. They eat plants. They eat a lot in the spring, summer, and fall so they can stay alive in the winter when there aren't many plants.

Prairie dogs use their long, sharp claws to dig underground homes called burrows. Prairie dogs work together to dig a burrow. They dig tunnels that go to rooms in the burrow. Burrows have two holes, one to go in and one to go out, just like front and back doors.

Prairie dogs will bark in a high voice to warn others of danger. Other prairie dogs will then stop and sit up to look and listen for another bark. When prairie dogs are afraid, they run to their burrows. They stop inside the room closest to the opening. This is the listening room. They wait and listen. When it is safe, they will go out and look.

Baby prairie dogs are called pups. They drink their mothers' milk. They start to grow fur when they are two or three weeks old. They are five weeks old when their eyes open.

Prairie dogs live in groups like a family. They eat, play, clean each other's fur, and even kiss members of their family.

Name _____

Directions: Think about what you know about dogs and what you read about prairie dogs on page 107. In the Venn diagram, write the numbers of the facts where each belongs.

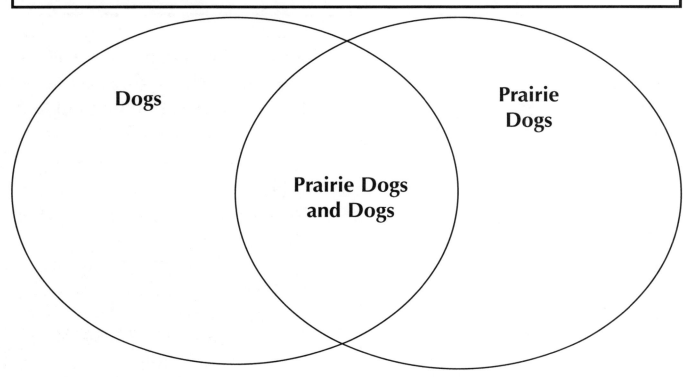

Dogs

Prairie Dogs and Dogs

Prairie Dogs

1. live in burrows
2. wag their tails
3. have long, sharp front teeth for eating plants
4. are rodents
5. kiss family members
6. can be led on leashes
7. drink mothers' milk
8. bark
9. eat meat-flavored dog food
10. have long, sharp claws that dig
11. have fur
12. go to a listening room when afraid

Name _____

Early Hot-Air Balloons

 One of the first hot-air balloons was made out of paper and cloth. The balloon was filled with smoke because people thought smoke would make the balloon rise. Buttons held the cloth together so the smoke would stay inside. The balloon floated up into the air.

The next hot-air balloon had a basket on the bottom of it. A sheep, a rooster, and a duck were put up in the basket to see if they could breathe high up in the sky. All of the animals were fine and landed safely.

Then a man went up in a hot-air balloon. He tied a wire from the balloon to the ground to make sure he would be safe. The balloon rose 85 feet (26 m) into the air.

Finally, a hot-air balloon with two men rose into the air with no wires holding it. It rose about 300 feet (90 m).

Directions: Draw a line to match a cause to its effect.

Cause	Effect
1. smoke filled the balloon	a. a wire was tied to the balloon
2. to see if they could breathe	b. the balloon rose 300 feet
3. to keep the man safe	c. the smoke could not get out
4. no wires held the balloon	d. the paper and cloth balloon rose
5. buttons held the cloth	e. animals went up in a basket

Name _____

Toll House Cookies

In the 1930s, Ruth Wakefield ran the Toll House Inn. This inn was located along the toll road between Boston and New Bedford, Massachusetts. One day Ruth wanted to make chocolate cookies but was out of baker's chocolate. Ruth was busy running the inn and could not stop to go to the store.

She broke some semi-sweetened chocolate into small pieces and added these to cookie dough. She thought the pieces would melt in the oven, and she would still have chocolate cookies. Ruth was surprised when she took the cookies out of the oven. The chocolate pieces had stayed in chunks.

Ruth had accidentally invented the chocolate chip cookie. The cookies were delicious. They were named Toll House cookies after the inn. The Nestle Corporation has this famous recipe on the back of each package of chips they sell. Chocolate chip cookies are probably the most popular cookies in America.

Directions: Use what you learned to answer the questions below.

1. Why did Ruth Wakefield put pieces of chocolate in her cookie dough?

   _____

2. Why didn't Ruth go to the store for baker's chocolate when she needed it?

   _____

3. What effect did the hot oven have on the chocolate pieces in the cookie dough?

   _____

4. Why were the cookies named Toll House cookies?

Name _____

A Poem

Poems are pieces of writing. Many poems have rhyming words.

Rhyming words are words that end with the same sounds or are from the same family.

Hat, cat, and bat are all words that rhyme.

Go, snow, and toe also rhyme.

Directions: Read the poem below. Circle the words that rhyme.

The Weather

The weather is strange,
Because it can change,
From hot to cold so fast.
The wind can blow,
Or it will snow,
But that will never last.
The weather is fun,
When up goes the sun,
But not when clouds fill the sky.
Snow and ice,
Are not as nice,
Coming down on the fly.
Dry or wet,
You can bet,
The weather will
always change!

Name _____

The Earth and Moon

Directions: Read about the Earth and moon. Then draw a line from each group of words to the correct picture or pictures they describe.

We live on the Earth. The Earth is in space. There are many other things in space. The moon is there. The moon is close to Earth.

The moon is not as big as the Earth. The Earth has a lot of water. There is no water on the moon. The Earth has plants and animals living on it. Nothing lives on the moon. In some places the Earth is green with trees, flowers, and grass. Only dust and rocks are on the moon.

People live on the Earth. No one lives on the moon. Men have visited the moon in spaceships. They have walked on the moon and returned with rocks and dust. Now people know more about the moon.

has grass, trees, and flowers

has people

has only rocks and dust

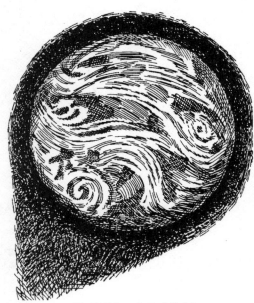

is in space

people live here

a man landed here to get rocks and dust

has no plants or animals

Name _____

Boa Constrictors

Boa constrictors are very big. They may grow up to 14 feet (4.3 meters) long. A boa kills its prey by squeezing it. Then the prey is swallowed.

Boas do not eat cows or other large animals. They do eat animals that are larger than their own heads. The bones in their jaws stretch so they can swallow small animals such as rodents and birds.

Boa constrictors hunt while hanging from trees. They watch for their prey. Then they attack. After eating, they may sleep for a week. Boas do not need to eat often. They can live without food for many months.

Boas are not poisonous. They defend themselves by striking and biting with their sharp teeth.

Boa constrictors give birth to live baby snakes. They do not lay eggs. They may have up to fifty baby snakes at one time.

Directions: Use facts from the story to help predict what will happen. Circle the letter of the correct answer.

1. A boa is hanging from a tree. Suddenly, a bird hops under it. The boa will ____.
   a. strike and bite it
   b. poison it, then eat it
   c. squeeze it, then swallow it
   d. sleep for one week

2. The boa is hungry and hunting for food. Which type of prey will the snake most likely eat?
   a. cow
   b. panther
   c. horse
   d. mouse

3. A boa constrictor is slithering through the grass. Out of the grass comes a hunter walking toward it. The boa will probably ____.
   a. strike the hunter
   b. squeeze and kill the hunter
   c. slither up a tree to sleep
   d. poison the hunter

Name _____

Porcupines

Directions: Read this story about porcupines. Use the information you read to help fill in the outline on page 115.

The North American porcupine is the only porcupine that lives in North America. These animals have brownish-white, needle-sharp quills. Quills are long, sharp hairs that have grown together. They can be 2–6 inches (5–15 cm) long. Quills are located under a thick coat of hair.

Porcupines use their quills when they are scared or threatened. Porcupines cannot shoot their quills. They hit their attackers with their quilled tails. The quills come out of the porcupine easily and stay in the attacker. New quills grow to replace the lost ones.

Porcupines are rodents. Rodents gnaw with their front teeth. A porcupine's front teeth continue to grow as long as the porcupine is alive. The North American porcupine lives in pine and fir forests. It eats bark and green vegetation. It may climb trees to strip bark from the upper parts of the tree. Sometimes this stripping kills the tree.

North American porcupines have very poor eyesight but can hear and smell well. They are nocturnal. This means that they sleep during the day and move around at night.

Baby porcupines are born with soft quills that harden in about one hour. They are called porcupettes and weigh 1 to 2 pounds (28 to 58 grams). Their eyes open after about ten days.

> **Directions:** Use the information you read on page 114 to complete the outline below.

I. North American porcupine

A. This is the only porcupine that lives in _____.

B. It lives in _____ and _____ forests.

II. All about the quills

A. Quills are brownish-white and _____.

B. Quills are _____ hairs that have grown together.

C. Quills can be _____ (5–15 cm) long.

D. Quills _____ be shot.

E. Quills easily _____ and stay in the attacker.

F. New quills _____ lost ones.

III. Porcupines are rodents

A. Porcupines _____ with their front teeth.

B. Porcupine _____ grow as long as the porcupine is alive.

C. Porcupines eat _____ and _____.

D. Porcupines have poor eyesight but can _____ and _____ quite well.

E. Porcupines are _____. This means they sleep during the day and move about at night.

IV. About porcupine babies

A. Porcupine babies are called _____.

B. Porcupine babies are born with _____ that soon harden.

C. At birth, porcupines weigh _____ pounds.

D. A porcupette's _____ in about ten days.

Camels

Directions: Read about camels and then finish the outline on page 117.

It's easy to know you are looking at a camel because of its hump. The Arabian camel has one hump and the Bactrian camel has two. These humps do not store water. Humps are a built-in food supply. They store fat that gives energy if the food supply is short.

Camels work for people in many ways. They pull plows, turn water wheels, and carry heavy loads. Camels are a source of transportation. People may drink camel's milk and make cheese with the milk. The meat of young camels can be eaten, but it is tough. The fat from the hump is melted and used as butter.

The woolly fur of the camel is woven into warm blankets and cloth. The cloth is used to make tents and clothing. The tough skin of the camel is made into strong leather for shoes, water bags, and packsaddles. Dried bones are carved into jewelry and utensils. Camel droppings are sometimes dried and used as fuel.

Camels can go days or even weeks without water. How much they drink depends on the time of year. They drink less in winter than in summer. The camel takes water from its food and keeps most of it in its body. A camel does not sweat to cool its body. The camel's temperature will rise in the heat of the day and cool at night.

Long, curly eyelashes keep out desert sand and protect the camel's large eyes. Thick eyebrows shade the camel's eyes from the sun. The camel can also shut its nostrils and lips to keep out blowing sand.

Many animals, such as cows and horses, walk on hoofs. A camel walks on a wide pad that connects two long toes on each foot. The pad spreads when the camel steps on it. This pad supports the camel on loose sand just as a snowshoe helps a person walk on snow. Their feet make almost no sound.

Name _____

> **Directions:** Look at page 116 to help you take notes about the camel.

I. Kinds of camels

A. _____   B. _____

II. How camels work for man

A. _____

B. _____

C. _____

D. _____

III. Products that come from camels

A. _____

B. _____

C. _____

D. _____

E. _____

F. _____

IV. The camel's body

A. The hump

1. _____

2. _____

B. The head

1. The eyes _____

2. The nostrils _____

C. The feet

1. _____

2. _____

Name _____

American Bison

Directions: Read about the American bison and use the facts for page 119.

One of the world's largest mammals is the American bison. Bison once roamed the plains of North America in very large herds.

Adult male bison are about 6 feet (180 cm) tall from the ground to the hump on their shoulders. They weigh about 1,800 pounds (810 kg). They are called bulls.

Female bison are called cows. They are smaller than bulls, weighing about 800 to 1,000 pounds (360 to 450 kg). From the ground to its hump, the cow stands about 5 feet (150 cm) tall.

Cows usually have their babies in April or May. The babies are called calves and weigh 30 to 40 pounds (13 to 18 kg) at birth.

Bison may eat more than 60 pounds (27 kg) of prairie grass a day. Both bulls and cows have horns. These horns curve upward toward their heads. Bison usually live 13 to 15 years. They may live up to 25 or 30 years.

The North American Indians used bows and arrows to kill bison. They used the bison to stay alive. They ate the meat; used the skins for clothing, blankets, and tepees; and made tools, utensils, and toys from bones and hooves. The Native Americans only killed as many bison as they needed.

During the 1800s, thousands of bison were killed to feed railroad workers. Bison were also killed for their skins. It became popular to shoot bison from moving trains. Often the dead bison were left untouched.

By 1900, only about 250 bison lived in North America. President Theodore Roosevelt helped to save the bison from dying out, or becoming extinct. Today the number of bison is growing, and they are no longer endangered. Bison may be seen in zoos. They are also found in national parks, wildlife refuges, and on private ranches.

Name _____

Directions: Complete this outline about American bison using page 118.

I. American Bison

   A. About the males

       1. _____

       2. _____

       3. _____

   B. About the females

       1. _____

       2. _____

       3. _____

   C. About the young

       1. _____

       2. _____

II. Interesting facts about the bison

   A. _____

   B. _____

   C. _____

III. Importance of the bison to Native American Indians

   A. _____

   B. _____

   C. _____

IV. Bison in the 1800s

   A. _____

   B. _____

   C. _____

V. Where are bison today?

   A. _____

   B. _____

   C. _____

   D. _____

Name _____

Australian Favorites

Directions: Read all about koalas and kangaroos and then turn to page 121.

Australia has many different animals. Two animals that live in Australia are the koala and the kangaroo.

Koalas look like teddy bears, but they are not bears. Koalas belong to a special group of mammals called marsupials. Marsupials have pouches used for carrying their babies.

Koalas are fussy eaters. They eat mostly eucalyptus leaves. Out of the 600 different kinds of eucalyptus growing in Australia, koalas will eat only the leaves of about thirty-five, most found in eastern Australia. A koala sniffs every leaf before eating it. If a leaf does not smell just right, a koala will not eat it.

Koalas spend most of their time in trees. Both their hands and feet have sharp claws. These claws are used for climbing and for cleaning their thick, fuzzy fur.

When a koala comes down from its tree, it walks with a swaying motion. If chased, it can run as fast as a rabbit. Koalas are also good swimmers.

The name kangaroo means "animal with big feet." Kangaroos are best known for their jumping or hopping. They move quickly and can hop for a long time. They are also powerful swimmers.

Kangaroos are plant eaters. They will eat food that other animals cannot. Because of this, kangaroos are found in all parts of Australia.

Kangaroos are marsupials. Like the koala, they have a special pouch where their young grow and develop. Later the babies rest or hide in the pouch if they are afraid.

A kangaroo's front paws are used like hands. They pick up food with them, use them to comb dirt out of their fur, and even lick them to clean their fur. Special claws on their back feet are also used to clean their fur.

Name _____

Directions: Use the story on page 120. Write the number of the facts below where they belong: in the koala, the kangaroo, or both.

1. live in Australia

2. eat only eucalyptus leaves

3. can swim

4. looks like a teddy bear

5. name means "animal with big feet"

6. use their claws for cleaning their fur

7. a marsupial

8. move quickly and can hop for a long time

Name _____

Muscles Are Movers

Directions: After reading about muscles, complete the details for the paragraphs. The paragraphs are numbered to help you.

1 Your body has more than 600 muscles. Exercise makes muscles bigger and stronger. Your muscles are at work all day long. They lift, push, and pull. Muscles work at night too.

2 Some muscles are called voluntary muscles. They move when you want them to move. Most movements use voluntary muscles. Raising your hand and stretching your legs to run are examples. The brain controls voluntary muscles.

3 Other muscles move or work for you. These are called involuntary muscles. Involuntary muscles work without you thinking about them. They work all of the time. Your heart pumps blood, and your intestines help digest food. These are examples of involuntary muscles.

Paragraph 1   Main Idea: Your muscles are at work.

Detail 1. _____

Detail 2. _____

Paragraph 2   Main Idea: Voluntary muscles move when you want them to move.

Detail 1. _____

Detail 2. _____

Paragraph 3   Main Idea: Involuntary muscles move without you thinking about them.

Detail 1. _____

Detail 2. _____

Answer Key

Turkeys 5
blue—are spotted
green—in trees at night
orange—are long
red—berries, nuts, seeds
yellow—a large bird

Modeling Dough 6
1. boil it
2. 1 tablespoon
3. mix with alum and oil
4. 2 1/2 cups
5. add food coloring
6. add to flour and salt mixture
7. until soft
8. store in an airtight container

Bears 9
Any facts from the story are acceptable.

Bike Safety 10
1. c   2. d
3. a   4. e
5. b

Killer Whales 11
1. circle birds; mammals
2. circle mountains; sea
3. circle blue; white
4. circle plants; meat
5. circle sleepy; smart

Foxes 12
1. d   2. b
3. f   4. c
5. g   6. e
7. a

Bird Beaks 13
1. finch/sparrow, cracker beak, seeds
2. flamingo, strainer beak, plants and shellfish
3. roseate spoonbill, spoon beak, shellfish, insects
4. heron, spear beak, fish and frogs

Boats 14
1. sailboat
2. fireboat
3. tugboat
4. rowboat
5. houseboat

Wart Hogs 15
1. tusks   2. root
3. thickets   4. warts
5. flee

Snow 16
snow—c
melts—d
snowstorm—e
blizzard—f
snowdrifts—a
snowbound—b

Flags 17–18
1. Texas
2. Alaska
3. Puerto Rico
4. District of Columbia
5. Tennessee
6. Alabama

Bird Facts 19–20
1. kiwi bird
2. emu
3. penguin
4. ostrich
Facts will vary.

What Is It? 21
1. football
2. golf
3. basketball
4. baseball

Hermit Crabs 22
1. hermit crab
2. in a shell
3. move to a new one
4. claw
5. another hermit crab

The Statue of Liberty 23
1. T   2. F
3. F   4. T
5. F   6. T
7. T

Venus Flytraps 24
Color the flowers with these facts:
The Venus flytrap's leaves have little hairs inside.
The sides of the leaf clap together.
The Venus flytrap is a plant.

Sticklebacks 25
1. stickleback fish
2. the male builds a nest
3. water plants and sticks
4. fight it off

Answer Key

Eagles **26**
1. large birds
2. small animals
3. live in the same nest for many years
4. one or two eggs
5. eaglets

Seals **27**
1. fish, shrimp, squid, krill
2. to help them move on land and water
3. oceans and on land
4. make barking sounds

Animals in the Winter...................**28–29**
1. Migration is when the animal leaves the home, returning when the temperature and/or food supply returns to normal. Hibernation is when the animal stays in the home, sleeping and living off stored body fat or small supplies of stored food.
2. Their bodies change to help them stay alive. Some grow extra fur to trap air, keeping them warm. Others change color to help them hide from predators.

Uncle Sam **30**
1. T	2. F
3. T	4. T
5. F	6. T

Icebergs **31**
1. ocean
2. water
3. ship
4. North Pole
5. iceberg

Sun Bears **32**
1. smallest
2. black
3. sun
4. claws
5. sticks
6. in the day
7. Malayan

Silkworms **33–34**
1. b
2. a
3. b
4. b

Apples **35**
Pictures should be based on the reading.

Hurricanes **36**
1. June, July, August, September
2. They do not live near the ocean.
3. They would know the safest times to schedule the trip.
4. No. The sun cannot warm the water enough to cause a hurricane.

Ounces, Pounds, Tons...................**37**
1. ounces
2. tons
3. pounds
4. ounces

Louis Braille **38**
I can read Braille.

Unusual Fish.................................**39**
Answers will vary.

Teddy Bear **40**
Answers will vary.

Magpies **41**
1. Answers will vary.
2. No. The magpie might steal from their nests.
3. The thorns may hurt animals trying to get to the nest.
4. for protection of eggs and the young birds

The Good Doctor **42–43**
Answers may vary.
1. They both know about medicines and illness.
2. A doctor works with humans, and a vet works with animals.
3. Both doctors must examine and decide what is wrong with the patient. Both recommend medicines and exercise as treatment.
4. Neither can communicate verbally.

Hedgehogs **44**
1. animal
2. pointed
3. fur
4. spines
5. ball

Walking Sticks **45**
1. stick, walks
2. insect
3. slowly
4. leaves
5. grows

Answer Key

Classifying **46**
    Toys: doll, truck, ball, paints, book, teddy bear
    Clothing: hat, shirt, mitten, shoe, shorts, sock

Baby Animal Names **47**
    Calf: elephant, whale, giraffe, cow
    Cub: lion, bear, tiger, fox
    Colt: horse, zebra, donkey

Baby Animal Names (cont.) **48**
    a. zebra and colt
    b. giraffe and calf
    c. tiger and cub
    d. elephant and calf
    e. horse and colt
    f. fox and cub

Shrews **49**
    1. large
    2. corn
    3. sleep
    4. dish
    5. water
    6. hair
    7. rain
    8. sun

Winter's Sleepers **50–51**
    True Hibernator:
    will shiver to warm itself
    hardly breathes at all
    seems more dead than alive
    body temperature drops below normal
    uses body fat while sleeping

    Light Sleeper:
    body temperature drops a little
    moves about and then goes back to sleep
    breathing slows
    easily awakens
    stores up food

Adjectives **52**
    Color: red, black, brown, white, blue, orange
    Size: large, small
    Number: three, four, two, one, six, many

All Animals **53**
    1. M   2. R
    3. B   4. B
    5. M   6. R
    7. B   8. M

Five Senses **54–55**
    eyes—sight

ears—hearing
nose—smell
tongue—taste
skin—touch
Favorites will vary.

Penguins **56**
    1. O   2. F
    3. F   4. F
    5. O   6. O
    7. O   8. F

Starfish **57**
    1. O   2. O
    3. F   4. O
    5. F   6. F

Figs **58**
    1. red   2. blue
    3. red   4. red
    5. red   6. blue
    7. red   8. blue

Neighbors to the South **59**
    1. fiesta
    2. Spanish
    3. Mexico
    4. peso
    5. maize

Ships **60**
    a. mast
    b. stern
    c. helm
    d. holds
    e. crow's nest
    f. bow

Totem Poles **61**
    feast—b. potlatch
    cut—d. carve
    tall, carved poles—c. totem poles
    the forest, animals, plants—e. nature
    friends that visit—a. guests

Daisy **62**
    Across
    2. girls   3. Daisy
    4. horses   5. plays
    Down
    1. place   2. Girl Scouts

Saguaro Cactus **63–64**
    Across
    3. expand   6. saguaro

Answer Key

7. deserts
Down
1. roots   2. needles
4. night   5. arms
8. egg

Vampire Bats 65–66
Across
6. fangs
7. nocturnal
10. wingspan
11. tablespoons
12. vampire
Down
1. heat sensors
2. round
3. echolocation
4. colonies
5. bats
8. roost
9. saliva

Manatees 67–68
1. e   2. c
3. d   4. f
5. g   6. a
7. h   8. b

Kites 69
down—up
high—low
black—white
round—square
work—play

Bark 70
thin—thick
smooth—rough
dark—light
outside—inside
top—bottom
sick—healthy

Ducks 71
This story is mostly about ducks. Color these eggs.
Ducks have two kinds of feathers.
Father ducks are called drakes.
Ducks are birds.
Baby ducks are called ducklings.

Animal Migration 72–73
Paragraph 1 Main Idea:
Many animals migrate to find food and to raise their young. Details will vary.
Paragraph 2 Main Idea:
Birds migrate south so they can find food.
Details will vary.
Paragraph 3 Main Idea:

Whales migrate to warm waters to raise their young.
Details will vary.
Paragraph 4 Main Idea:
Salmon migrate from fresh water to the ocean.
Details will vary.

Happy Birthday 74
birth day, every one, some times, some one, grown ups

Tomatoes 75–76
Answers will vary.

Honeybees 77–78
Answers will vary.

Skeletons 79–80
Answers will vary.

Skunks 81
Answers will vary.

Sleep 82–83
Answers will vary.

Verbs 84
birds—fly
rabbits—hop
dogs—run
mothers—mop
monkeys—climb
mice—hide
horses—walk
baby kangaroos—ride

Eating Right 85
Lunch Sack: milk, carrot, apple, bread, cheese, eggs
Trash Can: lollipop, soda, potato chips, cookies, cake

Alexander Graham Bell 86
creative, busy, talented, hard-working, smart, musical

Ida Lewis 87
1. loving
2. strong, brave
3. hard worker

Finding a Book 88
1. T, W   2. D, H
3. F, H   4. D, P
5. J, M   6. L, C
7. L, L   8. W, S

Encyclopedias 89
1. T   2. B

Answer Key

3. Q–R   4. M
5. D   6. F
7. N–O   8. T

Growing Bananas 90
1. c.   2. a   3. c

Jumbo...91
1. A special elephant was born in Africa.
2. He was soon sold to a zoo.
3. His name is Jumbo.
4. Jumbo was sold to a circus in the U.S.
5. Jumbo went to Canada.
6. Jumbo was hit by a train.

Archerfish..92
1. The archerfish sees the insect.
2. The archerfish shoots the insect.
3. The insect falls into the water.
4. The archerfish eats the insect.

Compass Rose 93
1. south   2. east
3. north   4. west

North America 94
1. Canada, United States, Mexico
2. Washington, D.C.
3. Answers will vary. San Francisco, Dallas
4. Pacific Ocean
5. Mexico
6. Mackenzie River

Rabbits 95
1. rabbits
2. plants
3. They eat trees and vegetation.
4. her body
5. kits

Mantids 96
1. it looks like it is praying when it is hunting
2. they hold its prey
3. they eat harmful insects
4. it is very hungry
5. changing colors

Marsupials 97
marsupials, pouch, carry babies, crawl, drinks milk
kangaroo, koala, opossum

Molting...98
Possible answers:
bird, loses feathers, loses one feather at a time
snake, loses skin, skin turns inside out

lobster, loses shell, happens many times

State Birds 99
1. robin   2. pelican
3. seven   4. four
5. New Hampshire

Money 100
1. Washington   2. half dollar
3. $100 bill   4. Lincoln, Jefferson, Washington
5. Lincoln Memorial

Candy 101–102
Answers will vary.

Dairy Cows....................................103
The food goes into the first two parts of the stomach. The cows brings the cud into her mouth and chews. She swallows the cud and it goes into the third and fourth parts of the stomach. The food is used to make milk.

Tulips 104
Tulips: 1, 2, 8, 9
Both: 3, 6,
Seed flowers: 4, 5, 7

Moths and Butterflies 105
Moths: 1, 4, 5
Both: 3, 6, 9
Butterflies: 2, 7, 8

Dugongs and Manatees 106
Dugongs: tusks, flat tail, does not migrate
Both: eat sea grass, blubber, two front flippers, endangered, mammals
Manatees: rounded tail, migrates, long whiskers, strong teeth

Prairie Dogs 107–108
Dogs: 6, 9   **Both:** 2, 5, 7, 8, 11
Prairie Dogs: 1, 3, 4, 10, 12

Early Hot-Air Balloons 109
1. d   2. e
3. a   4. b
5. c

Toll House Cookies.........................110
1. She ran out of baker's chocolate while making chocolate cookies.
2. Because she was busy running the inn.
3. The chocolate pieces did not melt into the batter.
4. Toll House was the name of the inn.

Answer Key

A Poem..111
strange—change
fast—last
blow—snow
fun—sun
sky—fly
ice—nice
wet—bet

The Earth and Moon.........................112
Earth:
is in space
has people
has grass, trees, flowers
people live here
Moon:
has only rocks and dust
is in space
has no plants or animals
a man landed here to get rocks and dust

Boa Constrictors...............................113
1. c.   2. d   3. a

Porcupines 114–115
I. A. North America
I. B. pine, fir
II. A. needle-sharp
II. B. long, sharp
II. C. 2–6 inches
II. D. cannot
II. E. come out
II. F. grow to replace
III. A. gnaw
III. B. front teeth
III. C. bark, vegetation
III. D. hear, smell
III. E. nocturnal
IV. A. porcupette
IV. B. soft quills
IV. C. 1–2
IV. D. eyes open

Camels 116–117
I. A. Arabian
I. B. Bactrian
II. A. Pull plows
II. B. Turn water wheels
II. C. Carry heavy loads
II. D. Transportation
III. A. Milk
III. B. Meat
III. C. Blankets
III. D. Cloth
III. E. Leather goods

III. F. Jewelry and utensils
IV. A. 1. does not carry water
2. stores fat
IV. B. 1. long, curly lashes and thick eyebrows
2. shut to keep out sand
IV. C. 1. long toes connected by broad pad
2. cushioned feet make no sound

American Bison 118–119
Wording may vary.
I. A. 1. six feet tall
2. 1,800 pounds
3. called bulls
B. 1. 800–1000 pounds
2. five feet tall
3. called cows
C. 1. born April or May
2. called calves
3. 30–40 pounds at birth
II. A. Eats more than sixty pounds of grass a day
B. Bulls and cows have horns
C. May live to be 25–30 years old
III. A. Ate meat
B. Skins for clothing, blankets, homes
C. Bones and hooves for tools
IV. A. Food for railroad workers
B. Killed for hides
C. Shot for sport
V. A. Zoos
B. National parks
C. Wildlife refuges
D. Private ranches

Australian Favorites 120–121
Koala: 1, 2, 3, 4, 6, 7
Kangaroo: 1, 3, 5, 6, 7, 8

Muscles Are Movers 122
Details may vary.
Paragraph 1:
Detail 1: Muscles lift, push, and pull.
Detail 2: Muscles work day and night.
Paragraph 2:
Detail 1: The brain controls this.
Detail 2: Raising hand is an example of this
Paragraph 3:
Detail 1: Heart beating
Detail 2: Food digestion